OUR STARS
OF
DESTINY

To the Eternal Oneness of All through Greater Knowledge
of the Light

OUR STARS
OF
DESTINY

Faith Javane

Whitford Press

ACKNOWLEDGMENTS

With loving gratitude to Edith L. Craig for her invaluable assistance in the preparation of this book and to Linda Stead for her unflagging confidence in me and my work.

Graphics and cover design by Joan Tilden.

Edited by Shawn C. Harriman.

Printed in the United States of America.
ISBN: 0-914918-92-3
Published by Whitford Press
A division of Schiffer Publishing, Ltd.
1469 Morstein Road, West Chester, Pennsylvania 19380

This book may be purchased from the publisher.
Please include $2.00 postage.
Try your bookstore first.

Contents

BOOK TWO

III. CONSTRUCTING YOUR PERSON PENTACLES

IV. BASIC ASTROLOGICAL RESOURCES FOR PENTACLE ANALYSIS

Foreword

"The aim of this book is to outline and delineate the journey of the soul." These were the first words of my last book and I can find no better beginning for this one, for the purpose I outlined then remains my purpose today; indeed it is the highest purpose any work can claim, and is the ultimate purpose I have dedicated my life to. In over fifty years of work toward this goal -- whether through private counseling, lecturing, teaching, or writing -- the focus has been the same. My attention has returned again and again to the divine potential of each individual. We originated in the divine consciousness, and our first breath and spark hold within a core cosmic seed. It is that seed that evolves through eternity to fulfill its destiny of reunion with God. The story of humanity is the story of this destiny and of our Quest for Higher Consciousness to attain it.

Every metaphysical science shares this knowledge, be it numerology, astrology, the Tarot, Biblical symbology, the Kabbalah, or any number of other studies. Throughout our history, we have discovered and refined these disciplines to help guide us in our Quest. These have not been static sciences; as we have progressed further along in our Quest, we have uncovered greater subtleties and deeper messages through advances in and syntheses of these various metaphysical systems. When humanity is ready, further esoteric features will be revealed.

We now stand at the Beginning of the Age of Aquarius, an Age that promises great spiritual advancement. In anticipation, the metaphysical sciences are adding new chapters of knowledge to their teachings. I have been privileged to be part of the preparations for this time of change. In two previous books, *13: Birth or Death?* and *The Master Numbers: Cycles of Divine Order,* I shared my insights on numerology. I extended the boundaries of standard numerological analysis to reflect higher number vibrations just now becoming widely activated.[1] I believe these advances have underscored the direction of humanity's further evolution and our potential for ever further advancement in our Quest for Higher Consciousness.

Similar advances await us in the other metaphysical sciences. This book focuses on one specific advance in esoteric Astrology -- the introduction and study of the Pentacle (Star of Destiny) and the Pentacle Aspects of the Horoscope. Going beyond the Pentacle, I also present sketches of the Higher, Many-Pointed Stars and the lessons they will bring into focus when humanity reaches a level to activate them.

This book will be open to several levels of interpretation. The person attracted to mundane astrology will find it novel and perhaps somewhat useful, but also rather "ethereal" and puzzling at times. Those more versed in philosophy and esoteric study will take to the techniques I presented with curiosity and enthusiasm. But in many ways, of course, this is not even a book about astrology. It is a book about Ultimate Purpose, about our Quest for Higher Consciousness as the path of return to the Divinity we all originated in. I hope it may awaken the reader to this potential in every person, and to confirm that deep-seated knowledge and wisdom we all possess.

---

1. Another book, *Numerology and the Divine Triangle*, presented a classic treatment of numerology as well as integrating it with facets of astrology and the Tarot.

Book One

I.

The Pentacle, Star of Destiny

ONE

Our Earthly Incarnation

The First Breath and Our Many Bodies

In each of us is the original spark of life, a tiny flame burning in the midst of dense matter. Its sustaining Force is not chemical but ethereal, and it is inhaled with every breath and converted into mental, emotional, and physical energy. It is like an invisible electrical energy flowing along the nerve fibers of our material bodies. Its rhythms, tides, and periods differ in each individual.

We sprang from the breath of Spirit, or God; only our form-bodies contain the "dust" of matter. We are thus Divine creations whose soul and spirit constantly breathes the higher ether or breath of God.

"And the Lord God formed man of the dust of the ground, and breathed into his nostrils the breath of life, and man became a living soul."

                                                      - Genesis 2:7 -

Our first breath begins our individual existence. It is the moment in which we become an ego, a self, an "I AM" consciousness with no counterpart elsewhere. Before that moment when the vital life-breath enters our bodies for the first time, we have no separate existence; we are merely a collection of cells living as a physical part of our mothers, whose breathing, circulation, and nurture have been responsible for our existence.

At our first breath, our physical birth, we are also each invested with an Etheric Body. Our Etheric Bodies exist both within our Physical Bodies and just beyond them, lying very close to our form. It is the Etheric Body that receives vibrations from outside us and translates them into the physical sensations like hearing and sight.

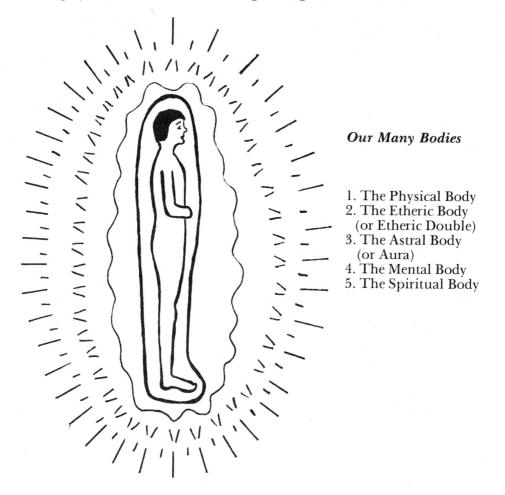

Our Many Bodies

1. The Physical Body
2. The Etheric Body
   (or Etheric Double)
3. The Astral Body
   (or Aura)
4. The Mental Body
5. The Spiritual Body

The above diagram is, of course, symbolic. All our bodies, all manifestations of the self, interpenetrate, for we are complex and integrated beings. Thus, the usage of words like "within" and "beyond" are used in a more metaphorical sense. There are even two further bodies not illustrated in the diagram, bodies that are truly without form and thus not depictable. They are the Emotional Body and the Celestial Body, and are discussed along with the other bodies in the section on the Seven Pointed Star. For more detail, consult *Man and His Bodies*, Annie Besant, Theosophical Publishing House, London, England, 1952.

Both the Physical and Etheric Bodies are sheathed in an Aura, or Astral Body, a force-field of protection that surrounds us in the shape of a "shell" or "egg" or "seed" - the shape of creation, of the birth of manifested form.

Our out-going emanations, as well as our incoming vibrations, come and go through our Auras; therefore, a clear and radiant Aura acts as a great asset to our daily lives.

"Every thought spoken or unspoken registers in our Auras, as does every expressed or unexpressed feeling."

- Dr. Julia Seton -[1]

Beyond the Aura lies the Mental Body, the region of thought. Thought is one of the more crucial tools we are given for our development. Right thought greatly sustains our Quest for Higher Consciousness, and baser thought greatly impedes it. Man is of four basic types of progressively higher thought patterns. Low types waste their lives in idleness, gossiping and leading unhealthful lifestyles. Average types earn their living, tend their homes, and enjoy the social life among their peers. High types, including teachers, clergy, reformers, and humanitarians, undertake a life of spiritual purity.[2] Super types - geniuses, Adepts, sages, and "illuminati" - are the most highly developed people on Earth, who live for the good of humanity and never restrict, hinder, or impose limitations on free and intensified lifestyles. The influence of the Mental Body thus increases with further growth and development.

The Astral and Mental Bodies work in close tandem. Thoughts express themselves as form, sound, and color in the Aura. The Aura constantly vibrates with thought activity, with the purer and higher thoughts producing lighter colors in the Aura. We thus walk around in a "sea" of ever-changing color, as the subtle thought substance of our Mental Body is constantly stirred by our individual thoughts.

The Aura of color also emits sounds which attract or repulse others according to the development of oneself and of the others. When we come into contact with others, our Auras touch and intermingle. This can help explain inter- personal attraction, as well as mass psychology (for with the mingling of Auras in a crowd of people, thought substance is readily passed from one person to another.)

Beyond the Mental Body lies the Spiritual Body. It is invisible, "super-physical," but is definitely felt by our "lower bodies." It is highly radiant, with an intensity dependent on the degree of glorification devoted to the soul's development.

We thus see again and again that the condition of each of our Bodies is predicated on the evolution of our Soul. Our first breath is not our beginning: the original spark that materializes then has a long history of development behind it, and our incarnation on to Earth is but one further step in our Quest for Higher consciousness.

This book will now share some new tools to promote that Quest, tools from the science of Astrology.

---

1. Dr. Julia Seton, *Your Aura and Your Keynote*, (New York: Column Publishing Co., 1912), p. 7.

2. Those who wished to follow the religious life were required to lead lives of purity and of following the Golden Rule. They believed that a transmutation of the creative energies within the body to serve a higher use was necessary for the safe passage of the "kundalini" up the spinal channel. They also believed that once "on the Path", a lower use of the creative power might be dangerous.

TWO

Astrology, Natal and Esoteric

At our first breath, the "picture of the heavens" is literally "stamped" upon our Etheric Body and on the blank corpuscles of the blood of our Physical Body. This becomes our Soul's pattern, its Horoscope, and is uniquely our own, just as are our fingerprints.

Our Horoscope, thus based on our moment of birth, the moment of our first breath, contains a vast amount of information. The belief in a definite relationship between one's Horoscope and one's destiny has persisted throughout history and holds a charm and everlasting allure to every individual. It is also the starting point of Natal Astrology.

Our Horoscope, or Birth-Chart, is a message. It gives a set of instructions outlining the best way to pursue our destiny.

To some, the Horoscope seems like a crystal ball that reveals every detail about oneself, past, present, and future. People consider it an illusive set of symbols that "know something" that we do not. But in reality, Horoscopes are tools that provide some answers, possibilities, and direction, and that show tendencies rather than make prophetic pronouncements.

Although Natal Astrology has most often been used for mundane purposes, it can also present deeper evaluations of ourselves. These deeper evaluations can enable us to choose goals within our reach and can show us how to take charge of our lives and work confidently towards future expansion and attainment. It shows us the best natural way to face any situation by interpreting the flow of vibration as best as our receptive abilities allow.

The Horoscope in Natal Astrology shows a way of mapping sequences of events and possible coming changes and thus gives us the opportunity to plan ahead as the movements of the Planets indicate. Symbols and aspects point to definite trends and to challenges that we can meet and solve at the proper time. Our Horoscopes thus present a plan of evolution which we may consult as we seek to make wise choices in behavior and right action.

The position of the Sun in our Birth-Chart indicates our lives' potentials and points to our future missions and goals. The Solar Chart shows the soul's attitude toward every department of life, as the underlying Natural Zodiac and House Rulers reveal. The Sun is the most magnetic of all influences in the Solar System and radiates a constant Spiritual Light. It is the source of all life on this planet; without it, there would be no plant, animal, or human life at all. It indicates our vital strength, our vibrant health, and all human conditions. Because this vital Force is flowing through our bodies, an understanding of its purpose is of profound importance in our lives.

Natal Astrology is expressed through a language of Symbols. Symbols may provide answers to conditions or suggest better ways of action to promote greater understanding of abstract qualities. A Birth-Chart carries a message through many personal-centered symbols, which may be better than words for communication when no other avenue is open:

The *Planets* show the energies that are operating.

The *Signs* show how the energies operate. From life to life the Soul incarnates in flesh bodies to fulfill the Plan of the Creator. A Soul is destined to learn and practice the highest spiritual truths. By being born in a certain *Sign* of the Zodiac, we learn the characteristics therein.

The *Houses* and *Aspects* show the areas of operation and point to conditions of what, why, where, how, and when they will be stimulated into active operation. The *Aspects* in particular indicate the idiosyncrasies of one's particular vitality, which are never the same as those of anyone else.

Esoteric Astrology builds on the foundation of Natal Astrology. It uses the same tools as Natal Astrology -the Planets, the Signs, the Houses, and such - but employs subtler interpretations of them and requires further meditation on its interpretations. Esoteric Astrology also adds more advanced tools, such as new Aspects and Fixed Star influences. Finally, its focus reaches far beyond a concern with the challenges and lessons of our life on earth, the domain of Natal Astrology. The ultimate purpose of Esoteric Astrology is to aid us in our Quest for Higher Consciousness.

Esoteric Astrology provides a deeper method of investigating the philosophical and Sacred Wisdom teachings which will fulfill the desire for Spiritual evolution toward Cosmic Consciousness. Every human being is like a microcosm in which all creative powers of the Macrocosm are being expressed in their individual potentiality.

Although the Birth-Chart shows the progress made, the individual has free will to choose whether to make the fullest use of the "Cosmic Gifts" or to cease to make an effort to improve his own Life-Pattern. But because the law of Justice operates in God's World, an individual will re-incarnate into conditions which have been earned (whether they be advantageous or burdensome) and which are patterned for constructive growth. No soul is released from the "wheel of birth and death" until it has evolved to a point beyond further need for mortal form.

As everyone is in a different stage of evolution, souls will proceed at their own level and pace in building their sense of Universality. Esoteric Astrology takes into account these significant individual differences, yet it also reveals similarities, the underlying unities expressed in humankind. Although we all respond differently to basic life experiences, we often do so within a set of typical, characteristic variations working beneath our surface consciousness. These variations can give new meaning to and impart a greatly desired security within the self.

To study Esoteric Astrology is thus to attain knowledge about ourselves, about what we are and what we may become.

We consist of Body, Soul, and Spirit.

To know the Body, to know the laws by which we can make it more vigorous, alert, and sensitive: study your Horoscope.

To know the Soul, to learn the laws by which the inner self can transcend the limitations of matter: examine the Moon in your Horoscope.

To know the Spirit, to learn the laws by which we may

come into conscious touch with the Divine Power, eternally immanent, omnipresent, omnipotent, and omniscient: look to the Sun in your Horoscope.

What degree of consciousness has the individual attained so far? This answer can be found and interpreted by every basic Astrological factor in a Birth-Chart. Not all factors will be relevant to everyone; this depends on the individual's present level of evolution.

In studying a Horoscope, the analyst must consider each Point, all of its Aspects, the Signs, the Houses, and every relation to other Planets that can be seen. The composite blend must be made, and again meditated upon. This must not be just a casual reading, but seen and put aside and then seen again and again. The analyst must interpret symbols in terms of their highest and innermost essence of meaning.

Different outlooks will come into your mind as you study your possibilities. This process of self-discovery can be intuitive, mysterious, vague, precise, joyous, or tantalizing.

In this process, the insights of Esoteric Astrology can allow us to "tune in" to greater levels of consciousness and new awareness and thus find new responses to our life patterns. The truth of Astrology thus offers greater guidance than any other known science. Through its study we can come to a clear understanding of ourselves. Self-knowledge is the key to Divine Knowledge, which propels us ever forward in evolution. No one can tell what we may yet discover, for there exists no limiting horizon that we may not reach beyond.

This book will summarize the currently available set of tools astrology employs to answer these and other questions, but it will focus on presenting a new set of tools - particularly the Five-Pointed Star of Destiny, or Pentacle. These tools, both old and new, will aid us through the symbols they reveal in our Quest for Higher Consciousness.

Part Four is a section on the basic facets of Esoteric Astrology. It gives only brief explanations and summaries of the facets and assumes some general familiarity with Astrology. Readers may desire to consult other books to get either an introduction to the discipline or a more detailed discussion of the facets. Several more specialized facets appear in Part Three.

THREE

The Pentacle, Star of Destiny

A New Dimension in Esoteric Astrology

A language of symbols underlies the Truths of the World's Sacred Scriptures. Symbols serve as teaching tools to explain the underlying meanings of our Plan and Purpose on Earth.

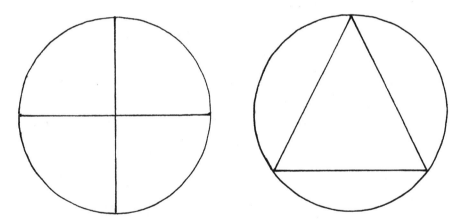

The CROSS represents humanity as "bearing the cross" of matter. The Cross within the Circle symbolizes the ever encompassing and ever-pervasive Spirit. It is also the oldest symbol representing the descent of Spirit into the limitation of matter.

The TRIANGLE, or trine within the Circle symbolizes the Spiritual Principle within us and within the "ALL". It symbolizes many Trinities important to esoteric studies, including body/soul/spirit, Father/Son/Holy Spirit, conscious/subconscious/Super-conscious, and love/light/wisdom.

The Cross and the Triangle have long been used in astrological analysis. Superimposed on the Horoscope, they reveal many often-obscured facets of our lives and our personalities.

The Pentacle, a Five-Pointed Star, is a more intricate symbol. It represents many aspects of our earthly incarnation; indeed, the Earth has many attachments to the number "5" as a Universal rhythmic quality. It consists of five continents, five oceans, five Elements,[1] five races, and five divisions of animals and insects. The individual as symbolized by the Pentacle has heretofore developed the five senses of Sight, Hearing, Taste, Scent, and Touch. Our very breath also relates to the "5," for we breathe at the rate of twelve breaths per minute, allotting five seconds to each breath. Also our normal pulse-rate is seventy-two beats per minute, seventy-two being the number of degrees in the Quintile Aspect (there being five Quintile Aspects in the circle of the Zodiac). The Pentacle is thus a definite symbol for the Human Being on Earth today. The greatness of its potential as an important symbol in the Zodiac and thus in astrological interpretation is equally definite.

This section will present the Pentacle as a new dimension of Esoteric Astrology. Although people usually respond to established patterns, an individual may become free by finding a way to break through the Zodiacal circle of limitations and thus "tap" a deeper source of life and consciousness. One can then touch the Cosmic awareness and rise ever higher toward the attainment of one's total potential.

There are great Cosmic Patterns that show the important steps in our evolution to the Point of union with Higher Self. I believe this new approach to the use of the Pentacle is such a pattern. The hidden meaning in symbols conceals or reveals the story of our evolution, the focus we are now working upon and the purpose of our unfoldment. Under this Symbol we may find the Points of our future state of illumination - our ultimate destiny.

Constructing our own Pentacles enables us to see the self before the SELF as it really is in the Universal Consciousness. This can give us a better understanding of the true purpose of our experience in the Earth Plane, and of what we are to accomplish by our lives here. Our Pentacles help to show the way by providing the answers to What, Why, Where, How, and When -thus we also call it the Star of Destiny. (see chapter "The Symbology of the Pentacle Points"). Pentacle aspects give creative imagination with ability to realize concrete results. Through probing and through testing the knowledge we acquire, we eventually come in contact with our Spiritual Selves and deepen our faith as we develop toward the Ultimate.

The Pentacle in the Horoscope points toward the Light, enabling one to evolve constructively, as the position of its points represent choices pertaining to the inherent Divine Love, Will, Wisdom, and Activity. It indicates, in a Cosmic sense, the power of the planets over the physical mind and body in its relation to the person as a potentially further developing Being. The Pentacle figure represents a cyclic process that will reveal a totality of conditions, circumstances, and experiences that one must encounter because of past actions. The Pentacle Points can show how to handle vibratory force by utilizing it to support our growing consciousness that knowledge and intellect evolve into intuition and wisdom and by producing a gradual change from the material nature to the Spiritual.

As we analyze our Pentacle Points, we shall find that the impulses of the Aquarian Age can penetrate within our depths and inaugurate a Divine process. This will occur first within the individual and then within the masses, The unknown within will thus become the known and the believed.

Accept your Cosmic Program, for your Spirit and Soul

has selected your *miracle formula*. Determine what your responses will be to the impact of this revelation. Your personal Pentacle presents a program for actualizing the promises of your Natal Horoscope in a most constructive pattern for growth and development, a high goal for the present incarnation. The SUN Pentacle Point and the other Celestial points can answer all your quests. You know now that you can choose your emergence from the mundane at your own timing.

Each of the Five Points of your personal Pentacle, your Star of Destiny, may reveal a new out-look as you meet each new challenge. Expect a further unfolding as you open your mind and heart to the infinite possibilities that await you.

Be aware of yourself and your environment - and "keep your aura radiant."

---

1. The elements of concern here are: Fire, Earth, Air, Water, and Light.

Four

The Pentacle and the Powers of the Higher Mind

The Pentacle was conceived of as a tool in Esoteric Astrology that we may use to further our understanding of our Higher Selves. Our Higher Selves are Spiritual Beings of Love, Light, and the Will-to-Good. We bear the compulsive urge to scale great heights, to excel, to be first. Our minds look ahead to further attainment as they begin to vibrate to a new and further level of responses. We draw energy through our Astral body from the Sun, Moon, and Planets, as well as from the Fixed-Stars in other constellations beyond the Zodiacal Belt.

The pentacle presents a pattern of that energy, a pattern we can use in our Quest for Higher Consciousness. It points the way to the blending with the LIGHT of the Higher Self, which may have been sleeping for centuries.

We can consider the five points of the Pentacle as an indication of a double awareness of the many facets of our potential. As we learn how to transcend earthly limitations, we need to believe in our ability to transform mundane desires and emotions into spiritual healing energies. We should try to contact our Cosmic Heritage and to eliminate our earthly bondage to mundane desires and glamor. We must not use an incarnation for the sole pursuit of materialistic pleasures and bodily appetites. We must seek to the depth of our beings for the answers to these higher octave points. The Etheric Points will become active when we reverently and consistently seek our goal or mission. We will need to apply all of our forces to create our own reality. We want to keep our energies moving in *spirals*, which are surprisingly powerful. (In early languages, the word for "spiral" and "spirit" was the same.)

The key word is vigilance. Inspiration will come as a result of our vigilant attention. The Soul's journey is long, and one must complete many incarnations to arrive at the destination of Cosmic Consciousness. We set our own limitations, even as we also promote our own progress. The "flow" of the Divine Light in the body seems to result in a kind of burning of the "Flame of Life," and while some may burn brightly, others may merely smoulder for lack of stimulation and inspiration.

We need not believe that we are chasing an illusive or intangible process of change, for we will become certain as our potentials become actualized. We will want to live henceforth from the creative spirit within us, for we have started on a quest for more vital meaning in our lives. We must begin with the heart for successful contemplation; "think with the heart -- feel with the mind." We should regard life through an ideal of self-less-ness. And we should love God first. Then the gift of vision will improve, followed by the strong desire for the Lighted Consciousness.

Five

The Symbology of the Pentacle Points

The What, Why, Where, How, and When of the Star of Destiny

The Pentacle represents our Destiny of the potential triumph of Spiritual Power over mundane materialism. It begins to emerge from the depths of our being, forming new energies through the Celestial Fire (Spirit) we are now touching. It works to transform our very substance; its blending represents the mastering of the four Elements: Fire, Earth, Air, and Water.

The Searching Self

Visualize the Pentacle Points placed upon your Horoscope. Imagine they are life-sized, and that the high point of the Pentacle is over the Divine Center in your head. Extend your arms so that the palms of the hands occupy two Pentacle Points; the other two Points hold the legs and feet. Visualize your body to be a body of LIGHT. Expand it, reaching into the Cosmos, then bring the Cosmic Energy back to your body, first to the aura, then to your heart. Now infuse the whole body with LIGHT, with thanks to God in praise of Oneness and Wholeness. These energies manifest themselves in our lives according to our own expanding development. Raise the egoic consciousness to that realm so that God-Consciousness may be fulfilled. If the latent gifts in the Pentacle Aspects are left unused, we are avoiding our Spiritual opportunities.

The GREAT WORK is to sublimate ourselves to the true Self within, as we are guided safely through our material existence.

"There are Celestial bodies, and bodies terrestrial, there is a natural body and there is a Spiritual body."

I Corinthians 15: 40-41...44

Each Point of the Pentacle symbolizes a question we ask as we undertake our GREAT WORK. To study these points is to gain greater insight into our Destiny - into WHAT, WHY, WHERE, HOW, and WHEN. This may seem simple but is not. Read through these questions slowly and quietly, in serene surroundings and with meditative countenance. You will find that it takes time and patience, but just approach these insights faithfully and understanding will follow.

DEFINING THE POINTS

WHAT

The search for God-Realization, the understanding of "I AM that I AM," is the conscious or unconscious pursuit of each and every one of us. A persistent search brings a source of Peace, harmony, and security; it becomes our very "Center," the Life of our life.

We may believe that we are not ready for a New Consciousness; "clinging to old habits and limiting ways" may seem more comfortable. But this new emergence need not be painful or too routinized - it can be an exciting and thrilling experience! We must just desire within our minds and souls to make union with God. We should realize "I AM the SELF, I AM infinite consciousness." We should live our resolve as a daily practice, placing our hearts in care of our Souls and knowing that our Souls' Quest is for the reality that God reveals.

WHY

The desire for understanding and Love, the idea that a source of perfect Light and Love can be kept active within, makes us feel secure and at peace. Light and warmth seem close to us and an unfolding sense of Peace and Love moves within our consciousness. A Love of humanity develops and surrounds us. As we awaken, a desire grows within for further exploration of this new "seed" idea, and for beginning a new project with much creative effort. We feel the need for fulfillment and growth; the desire grows, and a Pentacle Point suggests, "Believe: 'I AM that I AM radiating LOVE.'"

WHERE

We should learn to reach out beyond our former limitations. We can seek the CENTER within each of us that radiates Peace and Love and can employ our "seeing eyes" and our "hearing ears" to find the source of our goodness.

The SUN is the Key to our vitality. It is where the highest vibrational opportunities may appear, for we are starting on an incredible soul journey. We also look to Venus for our Love and sociality, to the Moon for our finer emotions, and to Mars for stamina and courage. We follow Mercury's intellect, reason, and practical decisions. We consult Saturn for stability, progress, and duty; Uranus for inspiration; and Jupiter for benevolence, philosophy, and philanthropy, and for our benefits and our good fortune. We seek Neptune for a sympathetic out-pouring of helpfulness for others, Pluto for regenerative and revolutionary change, Vulcan for the example of selfless service, and Earth for common sense in our conduct.

As we develop open and loving attitudes toward the world, we will feel a loving response. We can stretch our minds, our thinking, and our realization for Truth. As we search for beauty and goodness, we will forget hurts and fears and thus form a new attitude of constructive thinking and action. By gaining understanding of greater attainment, we will broaden our outlook to see beyond any shortcoming into security. We should develop a feeling of appreciation for a fortunate experience. As we begin to see good and beauty around us we will feel an uplifting and a joy in the sense of sight. Blessings are bound to accrue. As we become more convinced of the power of self-suggestion and inner imagery, it becomes easier to believe the extension of these techniques for the attainment of greater goals.

HOW

Whatever circumstances may surround us now, we will be helped and strengthened for HOW to find the answers to overcome any and all set-backs and challenges. Once we are "on the path," no book or teacher can take the place of our inner celestial selves. Our affirmations become a source of Divine certainty; we begin to choose how to increase favorable attributes, and how to discard old materialistic habits.

If our bodies seem to rebel, or our circumstances to irritate, we should say firmly to ourselves, "Peace, be still." We should let go of false beliefs, of old unwanted habits of negative behavior and do not dwell on the disappointments of the past. We should replace negative with positive and stretch our minds to understand more profound Truths and to grasp and hold on to Love and faith. And we must know that the inner Light is dynamic Living Power and seek more Love, Harmony, and Truth.

We should ask ourselves, "How am I unfolding? What experiences in my life bring the most harmony? How does this new sense of well-being affect the tenor of my life?" HOW we think about ourselves is most important because what we believe is sure to become manifest.

We may use research, cooperation, work, or many ways or means to attain our chosen goals. A suggested method of consistent study will show HOW to go on with the GREAT WORK of Transmutation. We should consider each Pentacle Point thoroughly. It is helpful to have a notebook to record progress. Keeping lists in this notebook is a most fruitful way to track involvement in our studies. After each study Point, a review of all Points will show us how far we have come since we began. If we re-read and ponder each Point, our understanding and expansion will surprise us. We should take time to be still and affirm, "I AM THAT I AM."

We will then discover that God exists in the midst of us as changeless eternal Spirit. Now we must find HOW to look inward and find the answers we have been seeking.

WHEN

Everything we desire to be can begin NOW! Future Spiritual growth is accomplished by building on our understanding of the present. If we live each day in the highest spiritual manner possible, then our present is blessed and our future is bright with promise.

We should dedicate ourselves to becoming all that we can be. WHEN we begin to investigate the ideal of our Pentacle, our Star of Destiny, something within us urges us to try a new way of thinking, a new way of life. We must lose the "little ego-self" in order to find the greater God-Self. We must choose to follow our Spiritual Destiny. The cycles of receiving and expressing are characteristic of all Spiritual growth. Life may seem chaotic at times, but in truth and in reality all is in Divine Order. We should determine not to have limiting thoughts, but rather to fill our minds with ideals of abundance. We then can look forward to the realization of Good and affirm the NOW-ness of all that IS.

"You therefore must be perfect, as your heavenly Father is perfect."

- Matthew 5:48 -

When we no longer accept illness, we have discovered the secret of Wholeness, and we will have a growing consciousness of the Oneness of all things. If we "catch ourselves" thinking that we are inadequate or lacking in some way, we ought to remind ourselves of what we know to be true of the "I" within each of us. We should refuse to believe in any self-weakness; rather, we should believe instead in our strength. In all cases of self-doubt, we must reverse our thoughts and affirm, "I turn within to my God, who is all powerful." This is *centering* on our inner being as having perfect control of all circumstances.

The God within is near at hand, reaching out as we reach inward. We can visualize and reach inward to the Central Super-Consciousness. Whatever limits us, we should visualize the LIVING, LOVING LIGHT as ever-present at our call. Once we have become convinced that we have attained that state of Consciousness, we can do anything we desire through our own Soul-power. This is the visualization of the God-Self within, through which all things are possible for the absolute Spirit - and the "I" within knows this! Whenever we awaken soul-power - at whatever age we may be - we have transformed our lives. Our first project is to improve ourselves. Therefore, we must do something NOW. We must not put off growing; there is danger in delay. Those teaching now were beginners once. SO LET US ALL BEGIN NOW!

Now that the Pentacle has come to our attention, we can accept our inner intuition that there is a "way" whereby we may realize the goal that has been our constant search. The prime desire within each of us is to search our Souls for their Mission in Life and to apply our Selves to best advantage. We will become more certain of the way as our potentials become actualized. And we can utilize the symbology of the Pentacle Points as aids in our Great Search for Actualization.

**The
Searching
Self
Turns
Within**

II.

Beyond
the Pentacle

SIX

Powers of the Higher Mind

The Quest for Higher Consciousness

The centerpiece of this book is the introduction, both on philosophical and practical levels, of the Star of Destiny Pentacle Aspects in the Horoscope. This will significantly augment the analytic power of Esoteric Astrology. This advancement of the science reflects humanity's further spiritual evolution, for the Pentacle Aspects present subtler insights into the issues that many of us now confront.

As humanity progresses even further in the Quest for Higher Consciousness, stars of even more points will become energized and take their rightful place in astrological science as tools for more refined analysis of the Horoscope. Already a few people have activated the Six-Pointed Star, and a very few have activated the Seven-Pointed Star.

We are all in the process of unfolding, of using our creative faculties and powers according to our own understanding. This process is directed from within and purposefully promotes activity which can culminate in beginnings of new and on-going Cycles of Spiritual growth. Once we have gained sufficient control of our presently-used five senses, we may develop even higher senses and further greater mental powers, with each additional octave of attainment endowing us with Divine and Celestial qualities - the Higher Powers of the Mind. Many of these Higher Powers have long been hidden in our hearts and souls awaiting the time of our awakening. One of these higher powers is *ORTHOCOGNITION* - a knowledge of the relationship between the conscious mind and the Numinous Element. Through Orthocognition we may experience an expansion of consciousness away from the self or ego and towards freedom, altruism, peace, and prosperity. Another of these powers, or reaches of the mind, is *LEVITATION*. The rising and keeping the body in the air without physical support, it is said to occur in states of spiritual ecstasy.

TRANSLATION, a power described in the Bible, is that power giving one the experience of transporting the body to the Heaven World without the death transition. Elijah, Enoch, and others were said to have ascended thus. Consult Gen. 5:24, II Kings 2:1, Hebrews 11:5, and John 6:62. Another higher power is that of *MIRACULOUS TOUCH*. It is attributed to Jesus when He touched Peter, thus enabling Peter to "walk on the water."[1] This is also called the laying on of the hands for healing. As we reach ever-higher levels of evolution and consciousness, as we activate the energies of each succeeding many-pointed star, these and other Higher Powers of the Mind come to lie within our grasp.

As presented here, the higher, or many-pointed stars are only briefly described. They present a symbolic path of evolution toward Higher Consciousness. Further evolution along this path will bring the higher stars into clearer focus and will require that astrology incorporate their influence into the Horoscope. Until that time, I present here a sketch of the path we might follow in our Quest for Higher Consciousness.

Life is the process of that Quest. It is a process of becoming - a great adventure to be expressed, a miracle of awe generating great astonishment, joy, and wonderment. We are on a spiritual journey with untold opportunities before us. On that journey we will learn to raise the focus of consciousness from the lower mind and personality up to soul awareness by drawing forth power for increasing responses and growth.

We must learn to use our bodies and minds to help us raise our consciousness. We must recognize the truth that all Creative Force lies within our bodies. This wonderful, fiery Force is the Life of our blood and of our very being. When this power is manifesting properly, we have absolutely no nervousness and we enjoy good health and restful sleep, never needing any drugs or stimulants. Everything seems to go well; we attain poise and relaxation with ease. To promote this, begin at the Spring Equinox to purify the body: abstain from stimulants and foods that cause gas, acid, or indigestion.

The Creative Force thus activated, referred to as the "Serpent-Fire," opens our sacred "Centers" as it ascends the spinal column and enters the brain as Light. This Light is the cause of the gleaming "halo" seen around some advanced souls. Although it is dangerous to open these "centers" before the body is ready, the "Spiritual Fire" rises and the centers open naturally once the body *is* prepared.

We must similarly prepare our minds. We must train our minds in concentration and Will-Power. The Powers and attributes of the Higher-Mind are reflected in all of us. If we examine all available teachings with open minds, if we examine every angle in them, then we shall learn celestial points not usually known or understood.

Development of each Star-Point produces the "seed" for higher consciousness within the next dimension, the next Star Point. As we continue our on-going progress, let each new Star-Point be sharpened with faith in the Great Work, which will bring us much fulfillment as cycles come and go. Let us keep our Star of Destiny, the Star of our personal inspiration, before our mind's eye, as we regulate our lives in anticipation of experiencing further enlightenment.

1. To " walk on the water" is a coded (symbolic) phrase meaning that the SOUL-POWERS (Subconsciousness, or water) will sustain you.

SEVEN

The Six-Pointed Star

The Star of Love and Intuition

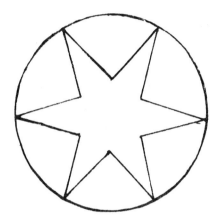

The Fire and Air Star

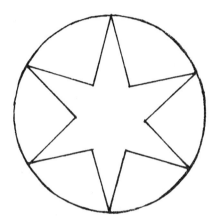

The Earth and Water Star

Soon humanity will be given the opportunity to evolve beyond even the many and wonderful dimensions offered by the Five-Pointed Star of Destiny. Our entrance into the Age of Aquarius will mark a "Great Leap Forward" in our intuitive abilities. Once the enlightened consciousness of the Sixth Sense of Intuition is more fully developed, we will be ready to share the Light. Humanitarianism will flow within us. The mundane sextiles of opportunity will have been grasped and will be used for unfoldment toward our greater goals.

The Horoscope will represent the development of intuition with two Six-Pointed stars. These two Stars represent the elements which are most harmonious with each other -Fire and Air, and Earth and Water. In the Aquarian Age, these Six-Pointed Stars will become the new symbols for Humanity - for we will have superseded the Five-Pointed Star of Destiny. We will have graduated from its influence, having mastered our five mundane senses and being no longer slaves to but rather masters of our emotions.

The Fire and Air Star

Without air, no fire can burn. Fire is the quality needed for "spark" and spirit, Air relates to the mental body and is the highest and most subtle of the Elements. Fire and Air bestow vitality, joy, and enthusiasm. The Signs and ruling Planets that make up the Fire and Air Star are the following:

Sign	Ruler	Quality
Aries	- Mars	- A proud and independent spirit.
Gemini	- Mercury	- Conscious mind, intellect.
Leo	- Sun, Jupiter	- Vitality, power, pride, pomp.
Libra	- Venus	- Peace, love and harmony.
Sagittarius	- Jupiter, Sun	- Jollity, religion, philosophy.
Aquarius	- Uranus	- Originality, surprise, creativity.

The coming Aquarian Age will witness the greater use of our Sixth Sense, leading to the attributes of mercy and justice. We will be Masters over the Elements, over matter, and over the atomic structure of our own bodies.

The Earth and Water Star

Without water, no seed could sprout or grow in the earth. The Earth and Water Elements endow the self with feelings and instinctive reactions as well as passion and inspiration for organized growth and success. The Signs and ruling Planets that make up the Earth and Water Star are the following:

Sign	Ruler	Quality
Taurus	- Venus, Earth	- Work in business and finance.
Cancer	- Moon	- Subconscious mind, emotions
Virgo	- Vulcan	- Selfless service
Scorpio	- Pluto	- Explosive energy.
Capricorn	- Saturn	- The business world, caution.
Pisces	- Neptune	- Mysticism, visions, dreams.

The coming Aquarian Age will see the "Christing of the Soul." We seek to give service to our fellow individuals, to our community, and to our World. As water has always symbolized the Soul, crystallized water - the snowflake - is the symbol of the "Christed Soul".

EIGHT

The Seven-Pointed Star

The Star of Symbolic Meaning

The Mystic Star

The Seven-Pointed Star is the Mystic Star, whose energy treats of creations not entirely of this world. The Mystic Star represents the Seven Gifts of the Holy Spirit: Wisdom, Knowledge, Healing, Prophecy, Tongues, Miracles, and Faith (I Corinthians 12:4-10). They represent the Soul's evolution beyond negative influences of pride, envy, wrath, avarice, sloth, lust, and greed. To gain insight into the use of the Seven Gifts, we must meditate on each one in turn. After we have found strength in the solitude and silence of meditation, we will awaken in the Soul to the mysteries of Divine Light. For meditation and chant, the use of the "OM" is best for body alignment and concentration. (The "OM" is said to be the first original sound uttered in any language.) Our communication between the Planes produces guidance for others also, and we may become teachers of Spiritual ethics. We learn to devote attention to our seven Soul-Senses, which are meant to give added powers over the Pentacle consciousness. Let your Soul reign over the senses, for Soulic-Energy-Mastery gives power for moving beyond material limitations.

The Seven Soul Senses

1. *TOUCH* gives the power to psychometrize.
2. *TASTE* gives the power to absorb and enjoy fine essences.
3. *SMELL* gives the power to distinguish the aromas of Nature.
4. *SIGHT* gives the power of clairvoyance.
5. *HEARING* gives power to receive etheric vibrations, clairaudience.
6. *INTUITION* gives the power to receive true inspiration.
7. *TELEPATHY* gives the power to communicate between the Planes.

Vibration is the nature of the fiery power which makes these gifts possible to attain and is the same power which is the source of all our strength towards Divine Purpose. "All things are from ONE, so all have their birth from this ONE THING by adaptation."

The Ageless Wisdom urges us not to accept unthinkingly but rather first to try. Thus it is said, "The only failure is the failure to *try*."

There are many other senses of which we should be aware:

The Danger Sense, located at the Solar Plexus, registers ahead of time and thus will warn of danger inside the body.

The Heat Sense is located in the heart, because the heart is responsible for body temperature. (98.6)

The Cold Sense is located in the spine.

The Pressure Sense is in the temples, which have a point which, if punctured, will release pressure and cause instant death. This warns in altitudes (high or low). If trouble occurs in the auricles or ventricles, the brain is notified through the temples.

The Hunger Sense is in the stomach. Blood governs the hunger sense and tells when it needs replenishing. Eat when hungry, because your blood needs rebuilding.

The Balance Sense is in the mastoid glands. If the mastoid is injured, one walks with a weaving gait.

The Rest or Sleep Sense is the whole brain. When this sense is active, the brain is inactive. Restive sense nullifies consciousness so that knowledge can be stored in the subconsciousness. (Our Cosmic storehouse is the ether itself. The Akashic Records, which are written on the ethers, record the history of creation and everything that has happened since.)

Behavior is the expression of these various senses. Through the use of intelligence, we can control our emotions and decide to what extent we are going to let our emotions govern our conduct. This is the way we form either good or bad habits -simply by control of our emotions. Therefore, try to find the higher wisdom of the senses while seeking to become aware of your SEVEN BODIES:

1. *The Physical Body* is subject to gravity and relates to health.

2. *The Etheric Body* relates to Etheric Planes above breath, space, and timing, and is invisible.

3. *The Astral Body* is luminous and full of Light-wisdom— the more Light, the more wisdom.

4. *The Mental Body* is energized thought patterns, experience, and memory.

5. *The Emotional Body* is one of sensitivities and is subject to electromagnetic forces, feeling, and sound.

6. *The Spiritual Body* is transcendental and relates to God-Force or Universal Energy.

7. *The Celestial Body* of heavenly Christ-like Substance is the sphere of the entire Universe.

Your higher Spiritual Body responds to the Light. Be still. Look within to evaluate your possibilities for deeper dimensions in consciousness. Cleanse your Temple-of-Thought; waste no time in trivia. Learn the difference between thought and consciousness. Consciousness is the ability to think, which develops through unity with the Christ-Mind.

NINE

The Eight-Pointed Star

The Star of Universal Rhythm

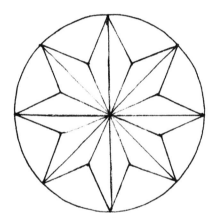

The Eight-Pointed Star

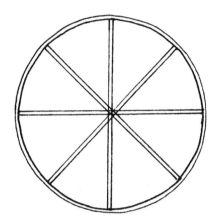

The Eight-Spoked Wheel

The Eight-Pointed Star and the Eight-Spoked Wheel are identical symbols of Universal Rhythm. They stand for the Rhythmic action of the fiery activity which sets the Life-Breath, or Holy-Spirit, in a whirling, wheeling motion throughout the Universe. They accommodate the whole panorama of events of the Eight Points and the Octagon and its trigrams within the Wheel. The horizontal Eight, ∞ the Cosmic Lemniscate, denotes Infinity and means the attainment of eternal qualities of Adeptship. The Eight Points of both Star and Wheel represent Solar Energy, which is within the vital breath of Life and Consciousness. The Eight-Pointed Star is the "Star-of-Light" and symbolizes re-generation, Baptism, and Universality.

TEN

The Nine-Pointed Star

The Star of Future Possibilities

The Nine-Pointed Star keys in to the more traditional meanings of the number Nine and points the way to the further points and the upper harmonies. This Star represents the NINE FRUITS of the Holy Spirit: Love, Joy, Peace, Patience, Gentleness, Goodness, Meekness, Temperance, and Hope of righteousness through faith. (Galatians 5:5, 22)

With many souls working on their own redemption, and pouring out wisdom and love to others, the World could soon be at peace. Our desire is for unity with God. Can the ideal of Harmonic Convergence change world consciousness? It could happen by a tremendous group effort exerting steady pressure and prayer for peace. We literally change the consciousness of the world every time we express soul qualities such as compassion and patience with everything that lives and breathes, and every time we express a caring or a kindness or a willingness to give time and resources to others less fortunate so that they can learn and grow.

The Power that redeems is LOVE. Its expression lies within the hearts and hands of all eager Aspirants. The unfoldment of the love-nature is that which opens the way to Higher Evolution.

We now reach out with patience, gentleness, meekness, goodness, and temperance to express each quality in our daily living and in relationships with others. Through faith in ourselves we experience peace and joy in the doing. We rise above the emotions of anger, appetite, lust, jealousy, and gluttony. Passion changes to compassion as we consciously realize our at-one-ment with Divine Substance.

ELEVEN

The Ten-Pointed Star

The Star of Spiritual Development

The Double Pentacle

The Ten-Pointed Star relates to the familiar glyph of the Tree-of-Life, a composite symbol created to represent the relationship between God and Man.

We live according to patterns. We cannot escape them. Astrology has the Horoscope; Numerology, the Divine Triangle; and the Tarot, its Major and Minor Arcana. All of these have many symbolic pictographs devised to help us understand ourselves.

The Tree-of-Life combines all these systems and adds a few more points, Trinities, and worlds of its own - seemingly the ultimate attempt at defining mankind. We use the "TREE" as a method of learning to think in symbols, for symbols are to the mind as tools are to the hand. These symbols are a system of Spiritual development. When we become able to learn through symbols and dreams, we will have learned a way of evolution for the Soul.

We can gain great insight by combining the ideas and values of the Ten-Pointed Star with the ten points of the Tree-of-Life. These Ten-Pointed patterns describe the Source of intelligence, the sustaining of Life, and the creative Will.

Creative energy is constantly emanating and penetrating through us here on Earth, where karmic and Cosmic Laws are worked out.

TWELVE

The Eleven-Pointed Star

The Star of Wisdom and Inspiration

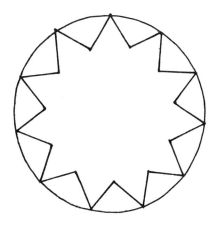

When man is able to respond to these higher vibrations, he develops ability to create new conditions, a new body, a new life, and a new consciousness - all in accordance with the Divine goal he has chosen. The "center" of the Eleven-Pointed Star therefore stands for the "still-point" that offers wisdom and inspiration. Its vibration reaches every atom of the body, as energy and substance are as one. Our Mind is our choice-maker, and we build according to our choices. We are greater than we appear to be, and by faithful and consistent effort and study we *can know this for ourselves.*

The development of the eleven points has produced an inspired teacher, an inspirational speaker, or a preacher whose wisdom and Light can be shared with the entire World. The perfecter of the "11" consciousness delights in giving loving service to all humanity and seeks to bring balance and harmony throughout the Earth.

THIRTEEN

The Twelve-Pointed Star

The Star of Exaltation

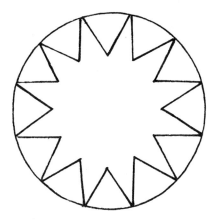

The Diamond Body

The soul within receives the Divine Energy, known as the Will-to-Good or the Will-to-God, and expresses it in human Growth-consciousness - in mental, emotional, and spiritual attainments. On this "Path" we have developed the Points outlined in previous chapters.

When the GREAT WORK of the Twelve-Pointed Star is complete, the crosses of matter become the exalted crowns of triumph. To win freedom from the "cross of matter" is to gain release from the bondage of the Earth Plane body.

The Twelve-Pointed Star is the symbol of the perfected Being. When we have experienced the lessons and established the qualities of the twelve points, we qualify as a full "Mahatma" or Great Soul. We have reached the "Omega Point" of the Aspect of Exaltation and will lovingly sacrifice ourselves for others, or become as a martyr for our ideals. We are consciously aware of the Omnipresence of the Omnipotent and Omniscient ONE. This is the birth of Cosmic Consciousness. We have realized the *"Blazing Star of Perfection!"*

Book Two

III.

Constructing Your Personal Pentacles

FOURTEEN

Meditation

As previously explained, the analysis of the Pentacle, your personal Star of Destiny, is a dimension in *esoteric* astrology. It is a tool for those seeking a deeper understanding of themselves. Therefore, a proper frame of mind is necessary when you undertake the construction of your own Pentacles. You will find that a sharp, receptive, and responsive mental state will greatly enhance your work. For this reason, I strongly suggest that you begin your work on your Pentacles with a prayer or a meditation. Perhaps you have a special prayer with great personal meaning; using this will "key you in" to your higher self. Or perhaps you wish to focus upon the new technique you are about to learn. For this purpose, I supply here a brief meditation or affirmation on the Star and our Quest.

I am a Child of God fulfilling my role in evolution. I am alive and eager for future development. I am on Earth here and now to open my consciousness, and to raise it in Quest of the ultimate Cosmic Consciousness which awaits us all. The Earth is my classroom, my laboratory, my workshop where I perform the great experiments of working toward that Cosmic Consciousness. The purpose of all my actions and of all my studies is the enhancement of this work. To this end, I aspire always for the best. I raise my consciousness to attain divinely ordered goals and to grow spiritually day by day. As my consciousness evolves, all my negative thoughts transmute into positive ones. I admit my faults and recognize my talents. I uncover my hidden abilities. I define my ideals and goals and work toward them.

I practice the Cosmic Laws of Order, Balance, Harmony, Faith, Patience, Love, and Compassion in all my thoughts and deeds. I experience the urge to live from the creative spirit within me, and the inspiration to search for ever-greater depth and meaning in my life.

I accept this as my Mission, my Cosmic Program, the Sacred Goal which is my constant search.

May my study of my Stars of Destiny serve as a path toward that goal. May they prove useful Cosmic Gifts and help me actualize the esoteric promises of my Horoscope. As I try to pierce through the mundane surface interpretations of my Horoscope, may they serve as "eyes of the spirit" and reveal the deeper realities of my life. May all challenges revealed provide a way toward my Goal.

May reflection upon my Stars foster my intuition and creativity. May my probing and testing help me come into greater contact with my Spiritual Self. May it enable me to see my own Soul-Self before the Greater Self that exists in the Universal Cosmic Consciousness.

I anticipate with great expectation the wonders my Stars of Destiny will reveal. May my Soul-Self interpret these wonders for me, providing answers to questions my mind has long been asking and encouraging action that directs me toward my ultimate goal.

As I study my Stars of Destiny, may I discover as my Divine Right my original unity, freedom, and immortality!

FIFTEEN

Specific Astrological Resources for Pentacle Analysis

—The Three-Fold Chart of the Individual

Before you begin your Pentacle analysis, you can gain a clearer concept of your Cosmic Gifts by compiling your three Horoscope Charts. These Charts depict the three parts of mind - the Super-Conscious, the Sub-Conscious, and the Conscious. Preparation of the three Charts presents us with a much richer field for study than would a single Chart.

Natural Zodiac Chart

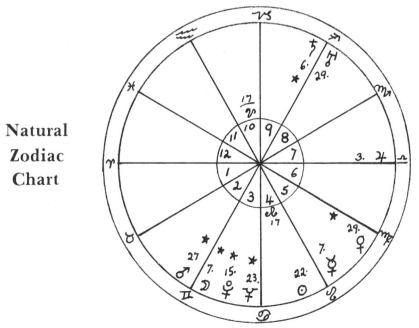

The first Chart is the Chart of the Super-Conscious Mind. It is a Natal Chart, compiled on a Natural or Universal Zodiac blank which has zero degrees on each cusp, beginning with Aries. Place the Sun in its Natural House at the Sign and degree shown at birth. This Chart predicts the mind that will function in our future and shows what Nature expects of us. It represents the Will-to-Live.

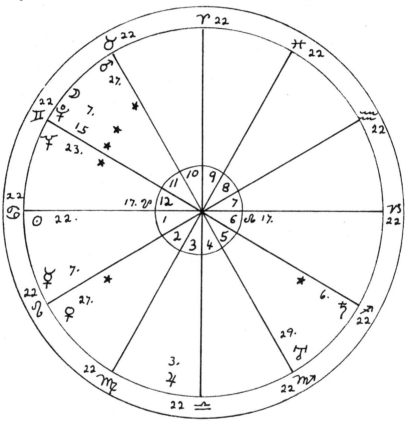

Solar Chart

The second Chart is the Chart of the Sub-Conscious Mind. It is a Solar Chart, starting with the Sun Sign, degree, and minute as the Ascendant. Use equal house cusp position with Sun degree as guide. When the birth time of day is not known, this Chart can be used as a valid Horoscope for the individual. It will show the Sign and degrees of all Planets and the natal

Aspects as well; however, the Moon's degree and the real Ascendant will not be accurate (as they will be in the third Chart). This Chart holds the memory of our past and shows what the Soul expects of us. It represents the Will-to-Love.

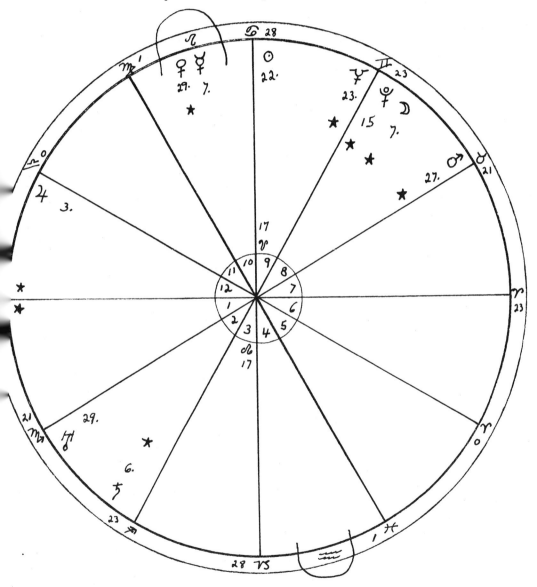

Time-adjusted Birth Chart

The third Chart is the Chart of the Conscious Mind. It is a Time-adjusted Birth Chart, based upon the date, time, and place of one's first breath as given on the birth certificate. Knowing one's birth time is a great asset because the Ascendant and degrees of the Planets are adjusted for an accurate presentation of the Horoscope; thus, this is the best working Chart. This Chart pertains to our present awareness and shows what you expect of yourself. It represents the Will-to-Good.

Once you have prepared each of your three Charts,[1] you will want to line up the Charts over each other as in the following diagram. The location of the Planets should be visible on all three Charts.[1] This will display the interaction of your three selves and permit a simultaneous, composite analysis of their features. You will be able to gain great insights into your place in evolution, the goals you are working to achieve, and the challenges you must overcome.

In beginning a composite analysis, it is important to note where the Fire Signs fall in each Chart, for they represent your spiritual side. Then you will be able to see all the influences bearing on the Natural Zodiac fire positions. In the above diagram, study sections showing the underlying influence of Mars, the ruler of Aries, the First House in the Natural Zodiac. Mars - your Planet of energy, expression, aggression, and action - activates the three-fold being and will underlie a decanate of each Fire Sign area of your Chart. The total vibrations bearing upon the affairs of those particular Houses will exhibit a mixture of Mars, the Sun, and Jupiter.[2]

If there are several Planets in your First House, the position of Mars will show where the action is in your life. Your Ascendant and First House represent your "persona," the device or "mask" you use in dealing with others.

In general, Planets show where things are happening. Signs are the principles the Planets work through. If you have many Planets in one House, the natural ruler of that House becomes highly sensitized. If a House is empty, it is not so strong, because a Planet is the focal point of attention. If there is a "singleton" (a Planet that stands apart from the others) or if there is only one Planet in an Element, analyze these features thoroughly. Aspects and Fixed Stars can be figured on all three Charts.

1. Everyone can use his Natal Chart and Solar Chart, because everyone knows his birth date. But because not everyone knows the exact time (hour and minute) of his first breath, not everyone can compile a Conscious Mind Chart. If you do not know your hour of birth, a competent Astrologer or Numerologist can in most cases rectify your Chart to a satisfactory degree.

2. Exception: If Aries is your Sun Sign and you have Aries on the Ascendant and Mars was in Aries at the time of your birth, you would have an emphasis wholly on Aries and Mars in the First House.

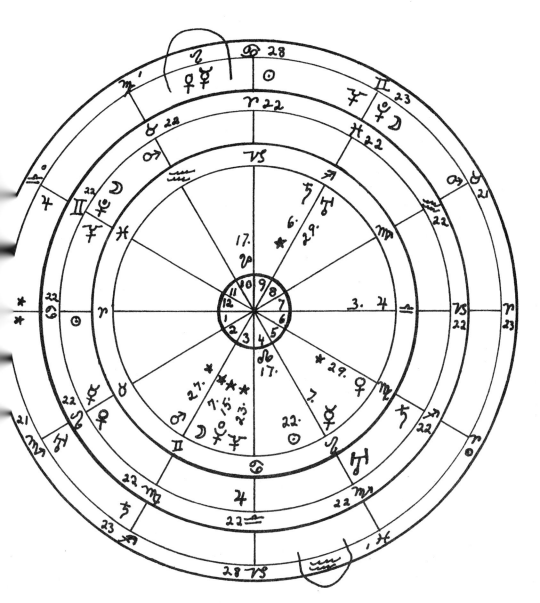

Three-fold Chart

—Special Aspects for Pentacle Analysis

The Pentacle, or Five-Pointed STAR OF DESTINY, symbolizes the Human Being with the five developed senses. The study of its Aspects enables an individual to experience subtleties of thought and new dimensions in consciousness, transcending the usual modes of experience and thereby easing many otherwise stressful conditions. It marks the possibility of one's emergence from the conscious mind level and of piercing the "upper" etheric levels of Spiritual vibrations at each of its Points. Used with the Main Aspects in the Horoscope, the Special Aspects can provide a deep and complete picture of the evolving individual.

SEMI-SEXTILE (30°)

This Aspect gives some advantage and may denote conditions developing, or coming to fruition through previous experiences during conscious awareness. Analyze Planets and houses involved for prominence and influence. Allow only a 1° orb.

DI-QUINTILE/DECILE (36°)

Another of the Aspects involved in the Pentacle. Allow only a 1° orb. This Aspect is more effective if it is part of other Quintile Aspects to do with the Pentacle, if the two Planets involved are part of a Mid-Point configuration, or if they are in mutual reception. It is an Aspect of the mental forces which confer insight into the secret workings of natural resources.

SEMI-SQUARE (45°)

This Aspect brings opportunities that often end disappointingly. It is a tension Aspect causing friction with others. Allow only a 1° orb.

QUINTILE (72°)

A Quintile is half-way between a Sextile (60°) and a Square (90°). Allow only a 1° orb. A Quintile involves non-congenial Elements with dissimilar Qualities. It is based on a symbolic five-fold division of the Zodiacal Circle, which may be connected by lines to form a Five-Pointed Star, the Pentacle. The Quintile can indicate talent or even genius. It confers originality and penetrating insight, giving ability to express thoughts and ideas and to bring them into manifestation, which may indicate literary or other artistic talents. If one is mathematically inclined, the Quintile gives the ability to solve problems for others. The Quintile also represents another "bond" which relates our physical selves to the etheric plane. It relates to man as a Star of Divine purpose in life. Several Quintiles, as in the Pentacle, could confer professional abilities and ambition leading to long-range work for the benefit of humanity.

BI-QUINTILE (144°)

This is equal to a Sextile if the Planets involved are favorable. Allow only a 1° orb. It is an aspect of occult and creative powers, which partakes of the mental nature of the Quintile. It can be associated with clairvoyance and keen perception which sometimes reveals details of past incarnations.

Clues and Directions for Interpretation and Development of Consciousness

The Quintile rules intuition. We refer to the Quintile as latent genius because when we listen to our inner selves, we are able to flow into a Oneness with the energies of the Planet's genius. When another Planet conjuncts a Pentacle Point, it tells of its importance in the further development of latent qualities and stimulates the urge to grow, expand, explore, and express talent. When Transits hit a Pentacle Point this signifies an opportunity to experience an external situation which can "trigger" new levels of consciousness. While Transits influence from the outside, Progressions stir us from within, bringing opportunity to express our internal urge to blend experiences of deeper awareness and freedom of expression.

SPECIAL ASPECTS SUMMARY CHART

SYMBOL	NAME	ANGLE	NATURE
⊻	Semi-Sextile	30°	Mildly good
Di-Q	Di-Quintile	36°	Resourceful
∠	Semi-Square	45°	Friction
Q	Quintile	72°	Talent
Bi-Q	Bi-Quintile	144°	Benefic

—Rarely-Used Aspects: "X Factors"

The Main Aspects and Special Aspects represent most but not all zodiacal Aspects useful to the astrologer. Sometimes a Chart fully delineated with the Main and Special Aspects remains puzzling. Some features may still be unclear, or the Chart may not reveal completely facets of one's life.

In such circumstances, one might profitably refer to the Rarely-Used Aspects. These could prove to be the "missing link" needed for full understanding of the self. The effects of each Rarely-Used Aspect are subtle, and are listed here for quick reference. Thorough definitions, explanations, and interpretations are available in other astrological texts, which can be consulted if one suspects that a Rarely-Used Aspect may be relevant to a chart.

INTERCEPTED SIGNS

An interception produces co-rulers of a House. Intercepted qualities lie latent until needed in some kind of crisis; thus, such qualities manifest themselves often only under stress.

PARALLELS (0°)

These Aspects are particularly subtle. They work quite slowly, and generally on the subconscious plane of awareness.

ASTEROIDS

Asteroids are currently being studied to determine their influence in the Chart. In general, they appear to be of imperfect implication and thus interfere with absolute accuracy in delineation.

CHIRON

One "asteroid," Chiron, is now acknowledged as a Planet. It is being thoroughly researched, and a Chiron Ephemeris has even been produced for the present century.[1] Chiron is said to be the key to our quest; indeed, an upright common key has been adopted for its symbol:(⚷). This is the Master Key made to unlock almost any common lock.[2]

NODES

Nodes denote our soul's desire as to the Karmic lessons to be resolved in the present life. They are links to the past and also point the way to the future.

The South Node symbolizes unfinished business from the past. This may seem negative or unfortunate but hardly need be so. Our past might, for instance, reflect positive behavior and many good works, which we would be fortunate to bring with us into our current incarnation.

The North Node represents promise that pulls us toward creating a better life. We seek always to improve ourselves, and we view each obstacle as an opportunity. Through dignified effort, we solve our problems and thus profit from them. We learn the lessons of love, forgiveness, faith, and right action.

1. It is now (October 1988) transiting the sign Cancer, where it indicates a movement for the return of the early principles of America-independence and freedom-and a renewed hope for true and sincere patriotism, civil rights, and international cooperation.

2. For further information on Chiron, consult *Chiron: The New Planet In Your Horoscope, The Key To Your Quest*, Richard Nolle, American Federation of Astrologers, Tempe, AZ, 1983; and issues of *Welcome To Planet Earth*, The Great Bear Press, Eugene, OR.

SIXTEEN

Basic Pentacle Analysis

Instructions

The instructions of the Basic Analysis are very brief. To help you understand them fully, a sample analysis will follow.

YOUR THREE-FOLD CHART

Prepare your Three-Fold Chart (refer to Chapter 15). Review its characteristic features; they will illuminate the interaction of your conscious, sub-conscious, and super-conscious selves and will give you a clear concept of your Cosmic Gifts.

YOUR STAR OF DESTINY
(SUN PENTACLE): CONSTRUCTION

Take your Universal or Natural Zodiac Chart. Locate the Sun in that Chart by Sign, Degree, and House. The Sun of your true self is your constant, and reveals the limitless potential of your individuality. The Sun's position in your Chart furnishes clues to the mystery of your vital Life Force. It will be the top point, or "Head Point," of your Star of Destiny.

Working from your Sun Head Point, count ahead every seventy-two degrees until you return to the Head Point. Write out your calculations to insure accuracy. These calculations mark the location of your five Star Points.

Mark all five Star Points on your Natural Zodiac Chart and connect them in the shape of a Five-Pointed Star. This is your Star of Destiny.

YOUR DOUBLE STAR
(SUN-MOON POLARITY)

Now locate the moon in your Chart (by Sign, Degree, and House). The Moon represents your personality - the mask you present to the world, your emotions, and your internal Soul-Self. Treating the position of the Moon as the Head Point, figure the location of each point of a Moon Pentacle, just as you did from your Sun position.

Take a new copy of your Natural Zodiac Chart. On this draw the Sun and Moon Pentacles together, with the Sun Pentacle drawn "on top of" the Moon Pentacle (see Example). This "Double Star" is a new means of visualizing the important Sun-Moon Polarity, one of the more basic and influential features of any Chart. The Sun and Moon are two great forces in your Chart, and their Polarity as represented by this Double Star brings into sharper focus many facets of both your outer personality and inner individuality.

Review the natures of both the Sun and the Moon as they appear in your Chart. Examine them in terms of Sign, Degree, Decanate, House, Element, Quality, and Season, and reflect on the combination of all these features.

Determine the relationship between the Head Points of the Sun and Moon Pentacles. Analyze this in terms of possible Aspects and in conjunction with the respective Houses the Head Points fall in.

Locate Saturn in your Chart and examine any Aspect it may form with the Moon or the Sun. This can be a very important Aspect, for Saturn represents the "Guiding Light" of your Chart.

YOUR STAR OF DESTINY: DELINEATION

Returning to your Sun Pentacle alone, note the basic features of the Head Point: its Decanate, House, Element, Quality, and Season. With this information you can begin to compile a "Table of Points and Aspects." Enter your information on the Table in the Point Description column.

Now examine the Head Point in terms of possible Aspects with Planets. (All Pentacle Points aspect each other as Quintiles or Bi-Quintiles, and should be noted only if a Point aspects a Planet.) Look for both Main and Special Aspects; if you feel it would be appropriate or needed, you may also search for Rarely-Used Aspects. Note each Planetary Aspect to a Point on your Table in the Aspect and Planet columns.

Note the basic features of each Aspect to the Head Point. These are the Position, House, Element, and Quality of each Planet that is in aspect. Enter this information on your Table in the appropriate columns.

Repeat the last three steps for each Pentacle Point until you have completed your Table.

TABLE OF POINTS AND ASPECTS

POINT	POINT DESCRIPTION	POINT ASPECTS					
		ASPECT	PLANET	POSITION	HOUSE	ELEMENT	QUALITY
F I R S T	Position: Decanate: House: Element: Quality: Season:						
S E C O N D	Position: Decanate: House: Element: Quality: Season:						
T H I R D	Position: Decanate: House: Element: Quality: Season:						
F O U R T H	Position: Decanate: House: Element: Quality: Season:						
F I F T H	Position: Decanate: House: Element: Quality: Season:						

To determine the Combined Element and Quality delineations, total the number of each type of Element and Quality from the respective columns on the Table. The most frequently appearing Element and Quality determines the delineation used. Refer to resource Chapter 27 for interpretation.

YOUR STAR OF DESTINY: ANALYSIS

With the information from your Table, reflect upon the significance of each Point and the Aspects each Point makes. This is the pinnacle of the many features of your Chart from the perspective of your Star of Destiny.

To add some final subtlety to your analysis, return to your Natural Zodiac Chart. Locate the Fixed Stars on it and write down the Pentad Statements for each of them. Meditate on these Statements in light of all you have learned as you have explored your Pentacle Points.

In closing, write down the Pentad Statements for each Pentacle Point. You may be surprised how well they summarize your Pentacle analysis.

After you have reflected on the meaning of each Statement, you can return to your Head Point. Taking into account all you have synthesized from the vast array of material available, and paying particular attention to the House your Head Point falls in, you might want to devise your own personal "Return to Head Point Statement." You can use this Statement as a motto to affirm your situation and goals in life. It is a product of your creative Spirit combining with your perceptive intellect - one of the many insights you have gained in your Pentacle Analysis.

BASIC PENTACLE ANALYSIS; INSTRUCTIONS

At this stage, you will begin to understand the wonders that your Star of Destiny reveals. If you have carefully studied your Chart in the past, you will notice that certain features have been brought into greater prominence by adding the tool of Pentacle Analysis to your basic astrological knowledge. A careful study of the significance of these newly-prominent features will prove them to be particularly useful guides for you in your Quest for Soul Development and Higher Consciousness.

SEVENTEEN

Basic Pentacle Analysis

Example and Commentary

THE THREE-FOLD CHART

Refer to Chapter 15. The Three-Fold Chart of the Individual for example Chart.

STAR OF DESTINY: CONSTRUCTION
Figuring Sun Pentacle Points

Sun Pentacle Calculations

Description of SUN Head Point:

Position: 22° Cancer		Element:	Water
Decanate: Third		Quality:	Cardinal
House: Fourth		Season:	Summer

Figuring of Pentacle Points:

<u>22</u> degrees of Cancer   =   Head Point

   8 remaining degrees of Cancer
+30 degrees of Leo
+30 degrees of Virgo
<u>+4 degrees of Libra</u>

(72 degrees)··· 4° Libra   =   Second Point

  26 remaining degrees of Libra
+30 degrees of Scorpio
<u>+16 degrees of Sagittarius</u>

(72 degrees)···16° Sagittarius   =   Third Point

Continued, next page

Sun Pentacle Calculations

Continued

14 remaining degrees of Sagittarius
+30 degrees of Capricorn
+28 degrees of Aquarius

(72 degrees)··· 28° Aquarius   =   Fourth Point

2 remaining degrees of Aquarius
+30 degrees of Pisces
+30 degrees of Aries
+10 degrees of Taurus

(72 degrees)··· 10° Taurus   =   Fifth Point

20 remaining degrees of Taurus
+30 degrees of Gemini
+22 degrees of Cancer

(72 degrees)··· 22° Cancer   =   Head Point

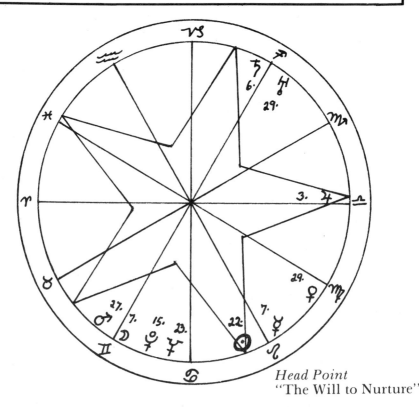

Head Point
"The Will to Nurture"

DOUBLE STAR (SUN-MOON POLARITY)
Figuring Moon Pentacle Points

Moon Pentacle Calculations

Description of MOON Head Point:

Position: 7° Gemini   Element: Air
Decanate: First   Quality: Mutable
House: Third   Season: Spring

Figuring of Pentacle Points:

7 Gemini · · · ·   7° Gemini   = Head Point
___

23 Gemini
30 Cancer
19 Leo
___
(72 degrees) · · · ·   19° Leo   = Second Point

11 Leo
30 Virgo
30 Libra
1 Scorpio
___
(72 degrees) · · · ·   1° Scorpio   = Third Point

29 Scorpio
30 Sagittarius
13 Capricorn
___
(72 degrees) · · · ·   13° Capricorn = Fourth Point

17 Capricorn
30 Aquarius
25 Pisces
___
(72 degrees) · · · ·   25° Pisces   = Fifth Point

5 Pisces
30 Aries
30 Taurus
7 Gemini
___
(72 degrees)

Double Star

Sun-Moon Polarity

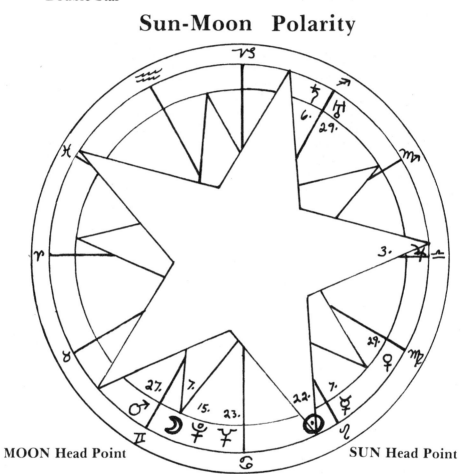

MOON Head Point   **SUN Head Point**

Commentary on Meaning of Sun and Moon

In all Charts, the contrast between the Sun and the Moon is striking. Symbolically, the Sun represents the conscious mind, reasoning and thought, individuality, and Spirit, while the Moon represents the Soul, the subconscious mind, and creative imagination. Also, the Sun reveals our place in evolution and the purpose of our present incarnation - the problems, challenges, gifts, and talents at our disposal. The Moon reveals our past, our "karmic debt" - our limitations and handicaps and work left unfinished, avoided, or refused in former lives. Physically, the Moon transits a House in about two and a half days, the Sun in about thirty. Thus, the Moon travels through the entire Zodiac - and is influenced by characterists of each House and Planet - every month; as a result, its nature is highly variable. The Sun, on the other hand, circles the Zodiac once a year; compared to that of the Moon, its influence is a relatively stable one. Thus, to examine the Pentacles of these two sets of influences in tandem is to add a rich, new dimension to your analysis.

In this particular Polarity, the Sun's position is in Cancer and indicates a focus on your surroundings, in particular the home. You are also concerned with a clean environment in your community and are patriotic about your country. You are protective of your home and work for stability and security there. You are self-reliant and in relationships flexible and adaptable. Finally, you are honest and loyal, a deep thinker with a strong sense of justice. Your aptitude with words inspires confidence in others. There is no limit to your potential achievements.

The Moon in this Polarity is in a Balsamic Phase. A Balsamic Moon is the last phase before the New Moon. It thus represents the greater part of the past and the weaker qualities of a Sign. But because it lies on the edge of a New Moon, it also indicates a readiness for a transformation of consciousness and creates the desire for a completely new future. This influence can even project inwardly to your greater Soul Goals and your next incarnation. This particular Balsamic Moon also is somewhat of a paradox, for it lies in the first Decanate of its Sign Gemini.

The Moon in this Polarity (in Gemini) indicates a sleeping talent marked by sensitive impressions, a good memory, and literary achievement. You should learn to concentrate your attention to prevent the diversion and scattering of your energies. But if you awaken your interest in achievement, nothing will impede your soul's intention.

Aspect between Sun and Moon

The distance between the Sun and Moon is 45 degrees-a Semi-Square Aspect. This is an Aspect of friction and tense emotions. The Moon lies in the Third House and the Sun in the Fourth. Thus, the friction could be between respective House characteristics of relatives and home, soul and body, sub-conscious mind and conscious choices, neighbors and parents, short trips and your environment, or personal communications and natural resources.

Saturn Aspects

In this Polarity, the Moon (Third House, Gemini, Air) forms an opposition to Saturn (Ninth House, Sagittarius, Fire). As you know, the Moon reveals facets of your past, often negative or karmic facets. These facets can be re-shaped by your Chart's guiding light as indicated by Saturn. Saturn shows you how to channel your energies away from earthly desires and toward your future attainments. But with the Moon and Saturn in opposition, that ideal mental harmony may be denied until you learn to turn inward, to bring your conscious mind into accord with the Super-conscious mind. This is a challenge that you alone can meet.

Star of Destiny: Delineation

Sun Pentacle

Refer to this chapter's "Star of Destiny: Construction" section to review the sample Sun Pentacle.

TABLE OF POINTS AND ASPECTS

POINT	POINT DESCRIPTION	POINT ASPECTS					
		ASPECT	PLANET	POSITION	HOUSE	ELEMENT	QUALITY
FIRST	Position: 22/♋	⚹	♄	23/♊	3rd	air	mutable
	Decanate: 3rd	D1 - Q	♇	15/♊	3rd	air	mutable
	House: 4th	D1 Q	♀	29/♌	5th	fire	fixed
	Element: water	∠	☽	7/♊	3rd	air	mutable
	Quality: cardinal	*	♂	27/♉	2nd	earth	fixed
	Season: summer	Q	♃	3/♎	7th	air	cardinal
		△	♅	29/♏	8th	water	fixed
SECOND	Position: 4/♎	♂	♃	3/♎	7th	air	cardinal
	Decanate: 1st	D1 - Q	♀	29/♌	5th	fire	fixed
	House: 7th	*	☿	7/♌	5th	fire	fixed
	Element: air	*	♄	6/♐	9th	fire	mutable
	Quality: cardinal	Q	☉	22/♋	4th	water	cardinal
	Season: autumn	△	☽	7/♊	3rd	air	mutable
THIRD	Position: 16/♐	Q	♃	3/♎	7th	air	cardinal
	Decanate: 2nd	B1 - Q	☉	22/♋	4th	water	cardinal
	House: 9th	☍	♇	15/♊	3rd	air	mutable
	Element: fire						
	Quality: mutable						
	Season: autumn						
FOURTH	Position: 28/♒	□	♂	27/♉	2nd	earth	fixed
	Decanate: 3rd	□	♅	29/♏	8th	water	fixed
	House: 11th	△	♄	23/♊	3rd	air	mutable
	Element: water		☉	22/♋	4th	water	cardinal
	Quality: mutable	B1 - Q	♃	3/♎	7th	air	cardinal
	Season: winter	B1 - Q	♀	29/♌	5th	fire	fixed
		☍					
FIFTH	Position: 10/♉	D1 - Q	♇	15/♊	3rd	air	mutable
	Decanate: 1st	∠	♄	23/♊	3rd	air	mutable
	House: 2nd	Q	☉	22/♋	4th	water	cardinal
	Element: earth	B1 - Q	♄	6/♐	9th	fire	mutable
	Quality: fixed	B1 - Q	♃	3/♎	7th	air	mutable
	Season: spring						*

Star of Destiny: Analysis

Analysis of Head Point

The Head Sun Point falls in Cancer, which is ruled by the Moon. Its Element is Water and its Quality is Cardinal; thus, here Water is represented in its natural state -- calm and unrippled. Cardinal Points express themselves as testing, getting control of your emotions, practicing justice and balance in relationships, and leading or pioneering new projects. Administration of projects that require conservative and responsible judgments will also test your ambition.

The Sun's position at the Third Decanate of Cancer opens up the whole Water Trinity for consideration. The Water Trinity represents states of consciousness relating to feelings and emotions. In addition to Cancer, Scorpio and Pisces are energized. Scorpio, ruled by Pluto, represents water in its fixed state - frozen and hard. It is opinionated and relates to secrecy and to the occult and its mysteries. Pisces, ruled by Neptune, stands for water in the mutable state - vaporous and foggy. Pisces is dreamy and illusory and can deal with poetry, music, and arts. Sorrows and sympathy often enter Pisces's realm. Pisces must also reckon with worry and anxiety.

The Sun Head Point lies in the Fourth House. This gives conditions involving home and domestic matters, lands and mines, real estate, and other fixed assets. Many intense desires and interests occur in these conditions.

The Season of the Sun Head Point is Summer. The Summer Season may relate to time, especially the adult years, or sometimes to the summer as the best time to plan and start new projects concerning your ideals and purposes.

Study and meditate on each attribute listed. You face a multitude of incidents and conditions, happenings which occur throughout life, and people to be reckoned with. You will need a lot of time and reflection to realize fully the truth of these implications. These considerations are not for you to pass over lightly. Do not hurry; give yourself the time and space to recognize the suggestions your Chart implies and to realize the best good from them.

Head Point Aspects

TABLE OF POINTS AND ASPECTS

POINT	POINT DESCRIPTION	POINT ASPECTS					
		ASPECT	PLANET	POSITION	HOUSE	ELEMENT	QUALITY
F I R S T	Position: 22/♋	⊻	♈	23/♊	3rd	air	mutable
	Decanate: 3rd	D1 - Q	♀	15/♊	3rd	air	mutable
	House: 4th	D1 - Q	♀	29/♌	5th	fire	fixed
	Element: water	∠	☽	7/♊	3rd	air	mutable
	Quality: cardinal	⚹	♂	27/♉	2nd	earth	fixed
	Season: summer	Q	♃	3/♎	7th	air	cardinal
		△	♅	29/♏	8th	water	fixed

Head Point Semi-Sextile Neptune -

This Aspect gives you a slight advantage or opportunity to gather strength for thinking of newly inspired goals. Neptune in Gemini points to affairs pertaining to relatives, communications, and conditions around your neighborhood. This Aspect can bring newness, which with the mutable quality of its vibrations can give you considerable flexibility in planning based on idealistic or vaguely suggested events.

Head Point Di-Quintile Pluto -

This Aspect adds a strong background of resourcefulness in springtime planning for later warm-weather activities.

Head Point Di-Quintile Venus -

The Fixed Fire combination here strengthens your position vis-a-vis public image. Your career may tend toward acting or speaking, or even teaching.

Head Point Semi-Square Moon -

This Aspect can produce emotional friction. You must learn to cope with relatives or neighbors if contention occurs in your environment. You can cultivate patience with problems, most of which may be temporary or even trivial. The Moon's rapid movement helps to resolve trifling irritations within a few days.

Head Point Sextile Mars -

This Aspect challenges your inherent drive to turn toward the spiritual in order to grasp the finer vibrations of your opportunities. You are provided with an incredible amount of energy, which should be used constructively. You have an inner motivation to "finish the job" ahead rather than to stop to eat or sleep. Although positive in your own opinions, the fluidity from the "water" of the Sun renders you open to suggestions from others; still, you entertain a persistent striving for success. Communication is easy for you and you work for mutual understanding among your peers. This Aspect also confers upon you the ability to teach or write.

Head Point Quintile Jupiter -

This is a significant Aspect because of the nature of the Planets concerned. The quality of a Cardinal Air/Cardinal Water combination strengthens the powerfully good vibration which Jupiter bestows wherever it is positioned. This Aspect also suggests friendly relationships and fortunate marriages or business partnerships replete with qualities of balance, right, and justice.

Head Point Trine Uranus -

Your need for freedom is strong. You seek after the truth and want to teach the lessons of the New Age to inspire, stimulate, and enlighten others. You need the unusual in your life, but you wonder, "can Aquarian needs be met wholly in this world?" Uranus seems to bestow a profound sense of purpose upon you. It can represent the advanced mental vibrations of an "initiate soul." This Aspect confirms the viability of these ideals and helps you strive constantly for your higher spiritual goals. Creative ideals abound, along with the urge to use them effectively. This Aspect "beaming" into the Eighth House specifically awakens affairs of that House; thus, you may experience confusion over wills, legacies, or the affairs of the dead. But this Trine will also help you assess values in their truest sense and to settle all affairs harmoniously. You were endowed with secrecy and extreme depth of thought at birth, and these attributes will serve you well.

Second Point Aspects

POINT DESCRIPTION	POINT ASPECTS					
	ASPECT	PLANET	POSITION	HOUSE	ELEMENT	QUALITY
Position: 4/♎	☌	♃	3/♎	7th	air	cardinal
Decanate: 1st	DI - Q	♀	29/♌	5th	fire	fixed
House: 7th	*	☿	7/♌	5th	fire	fixed
Element: air	*	♄	6/♐	9th	fire	mutable
Quality: cardinal	Q	☉	22/♋	4th	water	cardinal
Season: autumn	△	☽	7/♊	3rd	air	mutable

(The leftmost column is labeled vertically: P O I N T and S E C O N D)

Second Point Conjunct Jupiter -

This is a very strong destiny Aspect. It represents the ideals of balance, right, and justice. Optimism is an attribute of Jupiter, and when combined with the Venus ruled Libra, it gives expertise in communications and the creation of harmonious relationships in marriage, business, and general socializing. The goal for greater Light and understanding motivates your actions and reactions. You may tend to be overly indulgent in your affairs and thus must take care to avoid behavior that could be construed as martyrdom for a favorite cause. You should use protective attitudes against your adversaries and diplomacy in solving differences. You are probably involved with some aspect of public relations, and should guard against letting your enthusiasm become too effusive. You are equipped to give cheerful and expert guidance to young and old alike. Others will seek you out because of the "lift" you bestow upon them. Your popularity is evident in your many activities.

Second Point Di-Quintile Venus -

This Aspect indicates an avid impulse for education, possibly in acting, speaking, writing, or teaching. It encourages resourcefulness in finding ways and means to accomplish desired goals. Diplomacy in action is also a prominent characteristic here.

Second Point Sextile Mercury -

You are resourceful and thoughtful and have a well-organized outlook on life and the mechanics of living. The Star Point in Libra endows you with kindness when dealing with children or in romantic and sharing situations. Education in art or law may appeal to you; in any event, you are well-informed and capable. You enjoy debate, for you have a winning ability for keen and quick responses. You are a gatherer of information wherever you go, and may even carry a notebook about with you. Something new always holds your attention. You fraternize easily with others and your wit is often entertaining as well as instructive. Education appeals to you and you are always either studying or teaching. You are often called on to be a leader in gatherings or group activities. You can be either cheerful or serious, as the occasion demands. You are a comforting presence to many and a source of good advice.

Second Point Sextile Saturn -

This Aspect gives you great skill in planning so that your ideas have an excellent chance for success. You are not afraid of putting in the hard work and discipline to achieve your goals. You pride yourself on your conservative behavior. An interest in philosophy strengthens your beliefs in honesty and fairness. If circumstances permit, philanthropy would allow you to accrue dividends in your many activities, and would serve to enhance further endeavors. You could develop talent in literature, education, or even the ministry. You can dispense sound advice to all inquirers because you easily find reasonable solutions to difficult problems.

Second Point Quintile Sun -

This is a very helpful Aspect throughout life. Refer to the Second Point conjunct Jupiter.

Second Point Trine Moon -

Your emotions are at peak most of the time (for the Moon's phases change so often), but even in adverse aspecting periods, you remain tractable. You have talent for public relations because of your affable disposition. You are careful in financial affairs, your judgment is sound, and your values are formed with integrity. Your many relationships are made with honest and sincere intentions. All in all, this is a very good Aspect to have in your life.

Third Point Aspects

P O I N T	POINT DESCRIPTION	POINT ASPECTS					
		ASPECT	PLANET	POSITION	HOUSE	ELEMENT	QUALITY
T H I R D	Position: 16/ ♐	Q	♃	3/♎	7th	air	cardinal
	Decanate: 2nd	BI - Q	☉	22/♋	4th	water	cardinal
	House: 9th	8	♀	15/♊	3rd	air	mutable
	Element: fire						
	Quality: mutable						
	Season: autumn						

Third Point Quintile Jupiter -

This Aspect indicates that,you are a "doer" with an enthusiastic zeal to bring ideas to fruition. You have great promise for completing projects that you begin.

Third Point Bi-Quintile Sun -

This Aspect will alleviate the limitation of your Third Point separative opposition with Pluto, although it is from a wider orb, which somewhat diminishes its energy. Do not hurry to bring things to a climax; remember that "the wheels of the gods grind slowly, but they grind exceedingly fine." Here your spiritual powers begin to emerge because you are facing a deeper challenge. If you are concerned about your Third Point opposition, stop and do the Pentacle exercise as described in Chapter 5, "The Symbology of the Pentacle Points."

Third Point Opposition Pluto -

This Aspect warns in affairs of travel, communication, and publishing. You must not be too aggressive or insist on a single path to achievement, for there is no one ideal way to truth. Other ideals also exist, and your policy must be flexible. Gemini has at least two choices, although one may be deemed negative; however, it is better to do *something*, even if the choice might be to your own detriment. Indeed, limitations can provide you with important lessons. Try to relax and wait gracefully and patiently. A right time to push your ideals will eventually arise. Just pray hopefully.

Fourth Point Aspects

P O I N T	POINT DESCRIPTION	POINT ASPECTS					
		ASPECT	PLANET	POSITION	HOUSE	ELEMENT	QUALITY
F O U R T H	Position: 28/♒	□	♂	27/♉	2nd	earth	fixed
	Decanate: 3rd	□	♅	29/♏	8th	water	fixed
	House: 11th	△	♆	23/♊	3rd	air	mutable
	Element: water	Bi - Q	☉	22/♋	4th	water	cardinal
	Quality: mutable	Bi - Q	♃	3/♎	7th	air	cardinal
	Season: winter	☍	♀	29/♌	5th	fire	fixed

This is the area of your Chart revealing the greatest need for reform. As this Point falls on the empty Eleventh House of your Birth Chart, the Sign (Aquarius) and rulership (Uranus) indicate the crux of the situation. Also, because all of the Points, Planets, and Aspects occur in the Third Decanates (which open Fire, Earth, Air, and Water in all conditions for use or mis-use), this delineation must be analyzed thoroughly. Take all Points, Planets, and Aspects into account and contemplate deeply upon their significance.

Fourth Point Square Mars, and Fourth Point Square Uranus

Because the Point falls in Aquarius, ruled by Uranus, this is in essence "Uranus square Mars." Notice in the Natal Chart that Uranus is in opposition to Mars . Thus, this really shakes you with surprise (Uranus) and with your dynamic energy (Mars) in the stubborn sign of Taurus you are facing an extreme test! You may encounter a new and unexpected obstacle at every turn - until your intellect comes to your rescue by use of your redeeming trine.

Fourth Point Trine Neptune -

This good Aspect from the spiritual Planet Neptune works for you if you pray for God's help and reach out to grasp it. In other words, love and forgiveness and sacrifice of the ego-desires can overcome every problem when these "Golden Rule" laws are stressed as the Way. Neptune used in its highest sense can help you in all disturbing situations you may ever confront.

Fourth Point Bi-Quintile Sun -

This Aspect may awaken long-forgotten karma, and help in finding the will to overcome.

Fourth Point Bi-Quintile Jupiter -

This Aspect instills in you a pioneering passion for the work you have chosen. This so-called minor Aspect is indeed a fully beneficial influence in your life, helping you achieve your goals.

Fourth Point Opposition Venus -

This Aspect can reflect the pride of Leo. It must be conquered, and humility (the spiritual opposition) is the remedy. Be contrite and understand the opposing factors. Use cooperation instead of opposition in building new attributes.

Fourth Point T-Square

The combination of the two Squares and the Opposition makes a T-Square. This particular one is a Fixed T-Square, and is one of the more difficult configurations you can have. The need to overcome challenges looms very great, and you must be equally "fixed" in your determination not to allow "anything or anyone" to stand in the way of your progress. You need to review your life's problems and disappointments and to remember how you surmounted them, and you must now resolve that you will deal with future set-backs in a more cooperative and tolerant way. Meditate on your challenges and you will find the means to meet them.

You need not be overly dismayed at your set of Fourth Point Aspects. Remember that the purpose of your work is spiritual growth. Consider the opportunities offered by the Aspects, for they imply changes in consciousness. They can help us to change our thoughts to more positive ones, reversing their polarity from counter-clockwise (representing loss and disappointment) to clockwise (representing constructiveness and hopefulness). These Aspects can help you see beneath surface appearances to the underlying reality; indeed, they can help you see with "eyes of the Spirit" to guide you in making important decisions .

Never forget that our mission is for Divine Purpose, so that your manifested life is governed by your spiritual goals. With this joyous realization and attitude you may transform the seemingly very negative sides of the Aspects into great tools for soul growth.

Fifth Point Aspects

POINT	POINT DESCRIPTION	POINT ASPECTS					
		ASPECT	PLANET	POSITION	HOUSE	ELEMENT	QUALITY
F I F T H	Position: 10/♉	D1 - Q	♀	15/♊	3rd	air	mutable
	Decanate: 1st	∠	♆	23/♊	3rd	air	mutable
	House: 2nd	Q	☉	22/♋	4th	water	cardinal
	Element: earth	B1 - Q	♄	6/♐	9th	fire	mutable
	Quality: fixed	B1 - Q	♃	3/♎	7th	air	mutable
	Season: spring						

Fifth Point Di-Quintile Pluto -

Stability and determination to carry out plans for spring and summer projects .

Fifth Point Semi-Square Neptune -

This is a friction Aspect in which a Fixed Earth Point tries hard to deal with a Mutable Air spiritual and illusionary Planet. Neptune desires idealism while Taurus is practical and sensible - about as opposite as two ideas can be. Yet this must be resolved, and can be only by faith and prayer. Call again upon your marvelous inner resources and determine to succeed. Begin now without doubt or fear.

Fifth Point Quintile Sun -

This Aspect can bring you "down to earth" as you plan goals for speedy attainment. Although you are quick and active, you must remember to provide for the unexpected, for emergencies caused by a lack of time or money. Taurus is by nature patient but stubborn, slow and perhaps plodding; thus, you must take care to control your emotions, zeal, and speed. It is a great advantage for an enthusiastic soul to have at least some Earth consciousness, so be thankful and careful, and count your blessings all along the way.

Fifth Point Bi-Quintile Saturn -

This Aspect can be a beacon light illuminating a "safe passage" through all the storms of change. The materialistic Taurus needs to accept the qualities of philanthropy as much as possible. Make this adjustment as quickly as your consciousness allows. This means that you must develop compassion for others and follow your "guiding Light's" decree in order to bring out the best cooperative consequences for the end result of One-ness.

Fifth Point Bi-Quintile Jupiter -

This Aspect is a benefit indicating careful consideration. It shows keen perception regarding marriage partnerships and financial relationships. You must make your decisions wisely and ensure that all your dealings are fair and honest. Seek to bring justice into those situations and to demonstrate love and forgiveness.

COMBINED ELEMENT AND QUALITY INTERPRETATION

Total Elements and Qualities from Completed Table

Elements		Qualities	
Fire	6	Cardinal	8
Earth	2	Fixed	8
Air	13	Mutable	11
Water	6		

In this sample analysis the majority of Elements are in the AIR Signs and the majority of Qualities are Mutable. Therefore, this is a combination of keen intellectual ability and refined personality, with a possibility to develop in either scientific or literary fields. This combination also tends toward accounting, secretarial, or teaching professions. Much depends on the environment for best expression here.

Fixed Stars and Their Pentad Aspects

Algol, 25° Taurus - unfortunate, "must learn to be fruitful and forgiving."

Aldebaran, 9° Gemini - energetic, martial. "Change to positive and dynamic way of life."

Rigel, 16° Gemini - benevolence and fame. "Resonance has made its impact on mind and heart."

Betelgeuse, 28° Gemini - ingenuity and riches. "Accept His Will in Divine order and plan."

Regulus, 29° Leo - variable, like Jupiter and Mars. "Love is the fulfillment of the Law."

Spica, 23° Libra (Conjunct Ascendant on Time-Adusted Birth Chart) - bestows wealth, beauty, and art. "Develop your responses and choose the better way for all concerned."

Arcturus, 23° Libra (Conjunct Ascendant on Time Adjusted Birth Chart) - fortunate, bestows fame and honor. "Follow your Celestial Star Points."

Antares, 9° Sagittarius - a Red Giant Star, headstrong, like Mars. "A key to transcend time and space."

Star Point Pentad Statements

Head Point, 22° Cancer
   "Become a peace mediator for God."
Second Point, 4° Libra "Rise from
   body to soul by conscious awareness."
Third Point, 16° Sagittarius "Build your bridges
   from the mundane to the Spiritual."
Fourth Point, 28° Aquarius "To know that God is
   Love unifies all philosophies."
Fifth Point, 10° Taurus "The 'call' to
   illumination."

Return to Head Point Statement (Motto)

This particular return to the Head Point indicates a work for stabilization, quality conditions during your senior years, and readiness for transition. Contemplate the coming Aquarian Age Format - the time of the Christing of the Soul. Benefit by the qualities of each Planet and Aspect you have studied in this Pentacle Analysis. Aspire actively to your goal of Higher Consciousness,
   "A time to analyze all feelings and instinctual reactions."

Conclusion

This analysis has been a quest for a more complete understanding of ourselves. We have viewed ourselves in terms of our five senses and our emotions, as well as in terms of our more ultimate places in evolution and our ultimate destiny. We have probed the WHAT, WHERE, HOW, WHY, and WHEN of the blessings and challenges which come into our lives.

Recall the questions of the Search from the Star Points' symbology.

WHAT are we doing? Seeking the "I AM."

WHERE do we search? Beyond our former limited searches in our mundane Horoscopes and toward the Center, the God-conscious point within.

HOW do we search? By displacing old habits, by replacing negativity with positive, constructive concepts.

WHY do we search? To attain a feeling of peace, serenity, and Divine security within our selves.

WHEN do we search? We can begin NOW on our ever-continuing and ever-progressing Quest for Higher Consciousness.

This example pentacle analysis has well demonstrated how the Star of Destiny provides us with greater wisdom and understanding. Its amazing "modus operandi" and the creativity its analysis cultivates in us can reveal personal characteristics hitherto unknown, unrealized, or unfocused. It can thus help us attain our highest goals. This new wisdom and understanding will engender a truth that will inspire us to learn and practice successfully the love and altruism forecast for the coming Aquarian Age.

Through all our self-study, and in particular through the penetrating perceptiveness we gain from analyzing our Stars of Destiny, we shall come to realize and accept that our True Selves are capable of achieving any goal we may desire. It is by this discovery of the nature of our selves that we embark on the higher steps of our Quests.

"He who conquers the self is more mighty than he who takes a great city."

-Proverbs 16:32-

EIGHTEEN

Further Possibilities in Pentacle Analysis

—Head Star Point Placement

As you have seen by analyzing your SUN-Moon Polarity, your Star of Destiny with the SUN as Head Star Point is not your only Pentacle. Your horoscope actually contains many Pentacles. The different Pentacles reflect differing depths and facets of your personality, and thus can present a very subtle way of understanding yourself.

The Head Point of your Star of Destiny is of great importance in your analysis. It may be placed on the Horoscope at the location of the SUN or any of the Personal Planets (Mercury, Venus, and Mars). The selection of a particular Planet is based on which facets of yourself you feel predominate in your present incarnation or in your life at this time, *or* which facets you wish to develop or explore. This flexibility in choosing to emphasize different facets of one's life makes an even further variety and subtlety of analysis available to you.

The following explanations present which facets are illuminated by selecting different Pentacles, that is, by each possible placement of the Head Point. The next section, "Head Star Point Characteristics," will provide brief descriptions of Head Star Points by Planet *and* Sign.

SUN

You have already examined the SUN Pentacle (see the Basic Analysis). It concerns your vital life, dealing with your soul and your spiritual characteristics, as well as traits of pride, nobility, dignity, power, ambition, and at times even dictatorship.

MOON

The Moon Pentacle relates to your personality, your image in public, as well as of the subconscious mind, psychic powers, and magnetic attraction, as well as restlessness and a changeable nature. Because of this changeable nature, the Moon Pentacle is used only in conjunction with the SUN Pentacle in the SUN/Moon Polarity (see the Basic Analysis).

MERCURY

The Mercury Pentacle describes your intellectual life. It is an appropriate choice for examining a life marked by a striving for self-control, mental alertness, proper inner vision, wise and righteous judgment in all situations, attention to the small incidents and details of living, poised and steadfast thought, careful discrimination, assured intellectual pursuits, and the search for higher consciousness. On a weaker note, it may also concern inconstancy.

VENUS

The Venus Pentacle focuses upon facets of affection and desire in one's life. This includes matters of romance, luxury, vanity, and the desire for attention, pleasure, and possessions. It also indicates one who is too easily led. Analysis of the Venus Pentacle is appropriate if one's life is marked by these characteristics, and in general can show where a life of glamor and desire will lead.

MARS

The Mars Pentacle relates to one's passion, drive, perseverance, aggressiveness, and pursuit of courage and valor. It also indicates a potential for harshness.

—*Head Star Point Characteristics*

The Sun as Head Star Point

SUN in ARIES

The Will to Act.
Boldness, energy, power, control,
leadership, pioneering.

SUN in TAURUS

The Will to Persist.
Building, solidness, standards,
ecology, economy.

SUN in GEMINI

The Will to Communicate.
Deftness, cleverness, quick
intellect, eagerness for change.

SUN in CANCER

The Will to Nurture
Sensitivity, change, moodiness,
caring, healing, shyness with
firmness.

SUN in LEO

The Will to Be.
Bold action, drive, glorious and healing rays.

SUN in VIRGO

The Will to Serve.
Careful, thoroughness, discrimination,
analytical ability.

SUN in LIBRA

The Will to Harmonize.
Justice, quality ideals, valued judgment,
harmony, peace.

SUN in SCORPIO

The Will to Transmute.
Extreme desire for reform, management,
occultism, perception.

SUN in SAGITTARIUS

The Will to Wisdom.
Inspired philosophy, international
arbitration, idealism.

SUN in CAPRICORN

The Will to Succeed.
Great ambition, caution, foundation, science,
firmness.

SUN in AQUARIUS

The Will to Transcend.
Vision, invention, originality, eccentricity,
unpredictability.

SUN in PISCES

The Will to Peace.
Sympathy, understanding, sacrifice, music,
healing.

Mercury as Head Star Point

MERCURY in ARIES

The Will to Act.
Research, intellect, mediation, adventure,
exploration, good learning capacity,
versatility, adaptability.

MERCURY in TAURUS

The Will to Persist.
Competence, thoroughness, sensibility,
realistic outlook, deliberation.

MERCURY in GEMINI

The Will to Communicate.
Alertness, inquisitiveness, logic, fluency,
cleverness, problem solving.

MERCURY in CANCER

The Will to Nurture.
Sympathy, imagination, shyness with
firmness in personal matters, impressions.

MERCURY in LEO

The Will to Be.
Out-spoken-ness, emphasis, cheer,
optimism, resentment toward discipline
and limitation.

MERCURY in VIRGO

The Will to Serve.
Method, neatness, discrimination,
discernment and worry when difficulties
arise, cultivation of faith.

MERCURY in LIBRA

The Will to Harmonize.
Appreciation, thoughtfulness, adaptivity,
balance, seeming indecision, impulsiveness
instead of patience.

MERCURY in SCORPIO

The Will to Transmute.
Perception, penetration, subtlety, secrecy,
depth of thought implying mystery, psychic
influences that sway opinion and activities.

MERCURY in SAGITTARIUS

The Will to Wisdom.
Optimism, sincerity, abstract thought,
foresight as a Cosmic gift, helpfulness,
friendliness.

MERCURY in CAPRICORN

The Will to Succeed.
Serious rational thought, cautious ambition,
skepticism, deliberation and practicality in
action, desire to win by wits and cleverness.

MERCURY in AQUARIUS

The Will to Transcend.
Study, invention, original thought,
brilliance, eccentricity.

MERCURY in PISCES

The Will to Peace.
Psychic power, poetry, music, enjoyment of
art and literature, inspiration, intuition,
occasional dreaminess, tendency to build
castles of illusion when idle, need for active
mind regarding important affairs.

Venus as Head Star Point

VENUS in ARIES

The Will to Act.
Quick thought, decision, idealism, ardency, impulsiveness.

VENUS in TAURUS

The Will to Persist.
Responsiveness to physical attractions, romance, conventionality, financial security, materialism, stability, faith, interest in horticulture.

VENUS in GEMINI

The Will to Communicate.
Need for freedom, friendliness, thoughtfulness, generosity, detachment, desire for change, adventure, experience, natural curiosity, emotion more mental than tender.

VENUS in CANCER

The Will to Nurture.
Love of home, domesticity, receptiveness, secrecy, sensitivity, strong attachment to loved ones, need to learn to "let go," self indulgence but never wastefulness.

VENUS in LEO

The Will to Be.
Pride, romance, ardor, theatricality, desire to be noticed, loyalty in love, warmth, affection, social grace.

VENUS in VIRGO

The Will to Serve.
Neatness, analytical ability,
  discrimination, lack of demonstrativeness,
  desire to share work interest, search for
  health through good living habits, greatest
  likeliness of all Signs to stay single.

VENUS in LIBRA

The Will to Harmonize.
Attachments of extreme importance to
relationships, fair judgment, love of art
and beauty, responsibility in partnerships
and marriage.

VENUS in SCORPIO

The Will to Transmute.
Deep secrecy, emotion, passion, mysticism
if in second decanate, subjection to
extremes in changing conditions.

VENUS in SAGITTARIUS

The Will to Wisdom.
Idealism, humor, social emotions,
enjoyments of sports and the outdoors,
frank honesty, liberal thought,
philosophical nature.

VENUS in CAPRICORN

The Will to Succeed.
Reserved behavior, desire for security in
  love life or marriage partnership, care in
  relationships.

VENUS in AQUARIUS

The Will to Transcend.

Friendliness, popularity, preference for
many friends rather than commitment to
any individual, demand for freedom in
action, belief in freedom for others as well.

VENUS in PISCES

The Will to Peace.
Compassion, artistry, loving nature,
devotion to ideals, desire for well-
organized and harmonious home life.

Mars as Head Star Point

MARS in ARIES

The Will to Act.
Aggression, self-confidence, reliance,
independence, progressiveness, strength,
brave determination.

MARS in TAURUS

The Will to Persist.
Industry, perseverance, tenacity, protection
of the environment, care for the earth.

MARS in GEMINI

The Will to Communicate.
Liveliness, alertness, wittiness, tendency
towards sarcasm, easy accomplishment of
mechanical chores, penetrating
conversation.

MARS in CANCER

The Will to Nurture.
High emotion, tendency toward irritation
and sharpness in speech, tenacity in

getting work done, need to learn and accept
approaching new Aquarian concepts,
attachment to habit or traditional ideas.

MARS in LEO

The Will to Be.
Ambition egocentrism, arrogance,
 inflexibility, need to learn cooperation
and patience, use of pride as a defence
against imaginary threats, importance of
status image.

MARS in VIRGO

The Will to Serve.
Industry, practicality, helpfulness,
 obsession with the details of life, need to
recognize the genius that lies within,
concern with health.

MARS in LIBRA

The Will to Harmonize.
Cooperation, ardor, magnetism, search
 for approval from others, desire to
balance oneself with conditions of the
 environment.

MARS in SCORPIO

The Will to Transmute.
Courage, willfulness, persistence in
getting one's own way, depth of feeling
for "flight or fight," quick choice of
 direction to uphold truth in action.

MARS in SAGITTARIUS

The Will to Wisdom.
Spirit, independence, keen insight giving
 ability to take action, strong belief in
 mercy.

MARS in CAPRICORN

The Will to Succeed.
Authority, desire for control of all
situations, excessive thrift, great care and
conservativeness in financial matters,
building of strong foundations in any
field one is interested in, confidence with
caution.

MARS in AQUARIUS

The Will to Transcend.
Resolution, discipline, dependable group
leadership, rebellion, genius dictating
progress in action, humanitarian
aspirations acting as inspiration.

MARS in PISCES

The Will to Peace.
Emotion, passion, idealism, cooperation
superseding war in order to attain peace.

—*Planetary Pentacles: Instructions*

Take a new copy of your completed Natural Zodiac Chart.

Select which Planet you wish to have as Head Point. Locate that Planet on your Natural Zodiac Chart by Sign, and Degree.

Count ahead from the position of that Planet every seventy-two degrees. Write down your calculations. Connect these Points on your Chart to create a Pentacle.

Analyze the Head Point Planet by noting and interpreting its Decanate, House, Element, Quality, and Season.

Analyze this Pentacle in terms of Head Point Placement, Head Point Sign, and Head Point Characteristics. Reflect on these features and arrive at a composite description of the facet of your life that this Pentacle examines.

If you wish, you may delve deeper into the meanings and messages that this Pentacle presents. To do so, you would follow the procedure outlined in the Basic (Sun Pentacle) Analysis - the examination of each individual Pentacle Point, all Point Aspects, and Pentad Statements. (You would not, however, examine a Polarity as you did in your Basic Analysis.) As in the Basic Analysis, you could prepare a "Table of Points and Aspects" for this Pentacle to help guide your analysis.

But you need not reach this level of detail to gain a sufficient understanding of the nature of your Planetary Pentacles.

—*Planetary Pentacles: Examples*

MERCURY PENTACLE

Description of Mercury Head Point:

Position: 7° Leo	Element:	Fire
Decanate: First	Quality:	Fixed
House: Fifth	Season:	Summer

Figuring of Pentacle Points:

    7 Leo —   7° Leo   = Head Point

     23 Leo
     30 Virgo
     19 Libra

(=72 degrees) —   19° Libra   = Second Point

     11 Libra
     30 Scorpio
     30 Sagittarius
      1 Capricorn

(=72 degrees) —   1° Capricorn = Third Point

     29 Capricorn
     30 Aquarius
     13 Pisces

(=72 degrees) —   13° Pisces   = Fourth Point

     17 Pisces
     30 Aries
     25 Taurus

(=72 degrees) —   25° Taurus   = Fifth Point

      5 Taurus
     30 Gemini
     30 Cancer
      7 Leo

(=72 degrees)

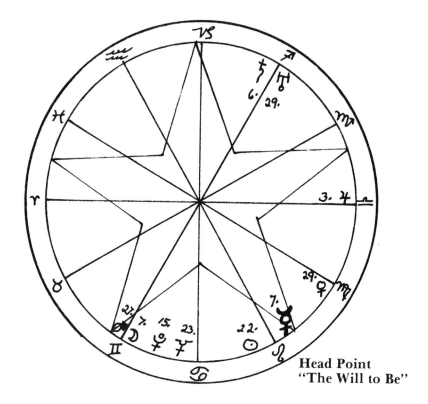

Head Point
"The Will to Be"

MERCURY PENTACLE

Commentary:

Mercury as Head Point shows the Will to Know and to Communicate. Mercury in Leo must use discrimination in developing methods to overcome proud or domineering attributes. Use your clear vision as protection and guidance. Lose no opportunity for kinship in communication, in particular in regard to philosophical and metaphysical matters. Do not push your beliefs upon others, but be willing to share your views when asked. Remember to practice cooperation through brotherhood and universal One-ness. Seek to serve others with your Light. Visualize your Will-to-Good center as vivified. Appreciate that a new way of thinking, a new perception can spark a dedication for service to humanity.

VENUS PENTACLE

Description of Venus Head Points:

Position: 29° Leo	Element: Fire
Decanate: Third	Quality: Fixed
House: Fifth	Season: Summer

Figuring of Pentacle Points:

29 Leo   29° Leo   = Head Point

1 Leo
30 Virgo
30 Libra
11 Scorpio
(=72 degrees)--   11° Scorpio   = Second Point

19 Scorpio
30 Sagittarius
23 Capricorn
(=72 degrees)--   23° Capricorn = Third Point

7 Capricorn
30 Aquarius
30 Pisces
5 Aries
(=72 degrees)--   5° Aries   = Fourth Point

25 Aries
30 Taurus
17 Gemini
(=72 degrees)--   17° Gemini   = Fifth Point

13 Gemini
30 Cancer
29 Leo
(=72 degrees)

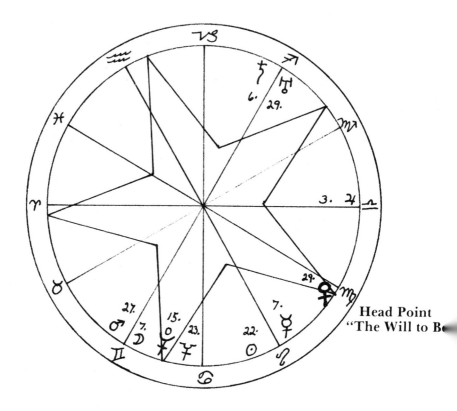

Head Point
"The Will to Be"

VENUS PENTACLE

Commentary:

Venus as Head Point shows the Will to Harmonize. In Leo it shows the will for power and desire for prominence. Desire is the source of much human suffering, for the selfish drive for personal wealth, beauty, ease, luxury, and glamor may occupy time which could be used in more constructive ways. Give up desire and be free! A way of liberation does exist - the way of love and sacrifice. Let your loving heart prevail and develop tenderness through consideration for others.

MARS PENTACLE

Description of Mars Head Point:

Position: 27° Taurus   Element: Earth
Decanate: Third   Quality: Fixed
House: Second   Season: Spring

Figuring of Pentacle Points:

27 Taurus — 27° Taurus   = Head Point

---

  3 Taurus
30 Gemini
30 Cancer
  9 Leo

(=72 degrees) — 9° Leo   = Second Point

21 Leo
30 Virgo
21 Libra

(=72 degrees) — 21° Libra   = Third Point

  9 Libra
30 Scorpio
30 Sagittarius
  3 Capricorn

(=72 degrees) — 3° Capricorn = Fourth Point

27 Capricorn
30 Aquarius
15 Pisces

(=72 degrees) — 15° Pisces   = Fifth Point

15 Pisces
30 Aries
27 Taurus

(=72 degrees)

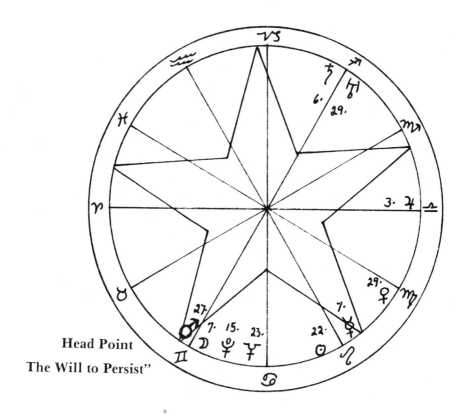

Head Point

The Will to Persist"

MARS PENTACLE

Commentary:

Mars as Head Point shows the Will to Achieve, to Act. The state of awareness coming from Mars is the striving for attainment as its aggressive pioneering spirits seek outlets for its dynamic energy. Although eager, you must learn patience. The earthiness of the Taurian energy seems to slow the ardor of the Mars persistence. You should seek to avoid clashes of temperament.

IV.

Basic Astrological Resources for Pentacle Analysis

Nineteen

The
Signs

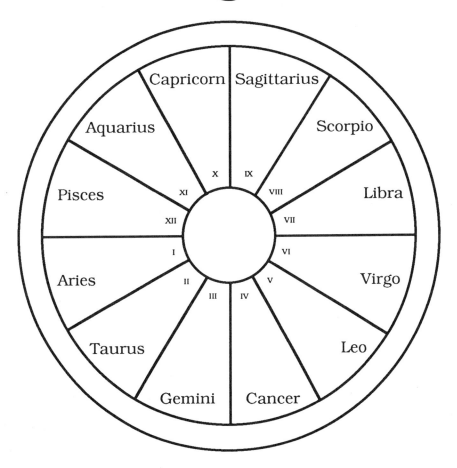

Esoteric Astrology addresses the progress of the soul during its incarnation on Earth. While we are in the body Freewill is completely dominant; the Earth is thus a sort of testing ground, or place of probation, for the soul, and whatever Sign of the Zodiac we are born into becomes the prominent lesson.

The Signs of the Zodiac indicate inherited traits, characteristics, abilities, and talents. These qualities are reflected in everything on Earth in terms of vibrational influences, and can be both Positive and Negative in action. This section describes the Signs only briefly, employing key words and phrases and in general stressing the positive facets.

The date of the Sun's entry into the Signs varies slightly from year to year; thus, the dates given are approximate. Only when you know the place and precise moment of your birth can you accurately determine your true Ascendant and the exact positions of the Moon and Planets.

If you are born "on the Cusp" - that is, close to the beginning or end of a Sign's period, you may be influenced also by the adjacent Sign. For a brief discussion of this, see this chapter's section on "The Cusps."

ARIES (March 21 - April 20)

Stand for the self, courageous and aggressive. Willful "bossy" types, selfish to advance their own egos. Ariens express much independence, vitality, daring, and impulsiveness. They are pioneers, ardent and energetic. They want their own way and domineer over others unless they are tempered by love and kindness. They must learn to control desires.

TAURUS (April 21 - May 21)

Show much determination, firmness, and endurance. Taurians move ahead moderately, with patience and caution. They are co-operative, slow to realize real values, and above all desirous of security. They are builders whose vice is inertia, and whose virtue is practical achievement and concrete success.

GEMINI (May 22 - June 21)

Dextrous and versatile, active and alert, their reasoning intellect delves deeply and has many interests. Geminis are unquenchable in desire to learn, to know, and to experiment, but they need to learn to discriminate and to make wise choices between the positive and the negative. They must watch reactions to friends, neighbors, and relatives. As Geminis embark upon an important phase in their lives, something they have not done before, they may analyze their situations in these ways: "I have a pretty good idea of my talents and I am using them fairly well" or "Sometimes I think I could do better, but my efforts seem adequate" or "I could do almost anything if I put my mind to it, but I don't get the time or the urge." This shows the trait of duality. The main weakness of Geminis may be being unresponsive and needing more incentive to go ahead spiritually.

CANCER (June 22 - July 23)

Tenacious, sensitive, kind, and nourishing, Cancerians are traditionally referred to as the Cosmic Mother. They have a reserved disposition but are adaptable to conditions and frugal for future provision. They are home-loving and industrious. Cancerians have tender feelings but should not allow feelings of guilt or remorse to reduce their efforts; they should be determined to dwell on thoughts of future goals.

LEO (July 24 - August 23)

Leos are proud and want their own high place in the Sun. Commanding, they enjoy rulership and dominion, and are magnanimous or Royal in personality. They express authority, boldness, and triumph, and also leadership, progressive attitudes, freedom to meet new challenges, and faith in self-worth. From the moment of birth, Leos devote tremendous energy (however unconsciously) toward creating an image acceptable to their ideal concept of themselves. They should work more to develop their "heart-side" toward others. Leos cater to the opposite sex.

VIRGO (August 24 - September 23)

Virgos thrive on responsibility. Industrious and helpful, they stick to system and order and are methodical, analytical, and thorough. They are efficient and practical in service to others and believe that brain is superior to brawn. Virgos have the ability to attain knowledge without difficulty. They are modest and conservative, particular as to hygiene, and flexible and open-minded with good power of observation. They may remain single and secluded, perhaps becoming a Hermit type.

LIBRA (September 24 - October 23)

Tactful, adaptable, balancing, Libras are loving peacemakers and understanding helpers. They maintain a balanced harmony under trying circumstances. Libras are usually courteous, pleasant, and agreeable, and also keenly perceptive, intuitive, and persistent.

SCORPIO (October 24 - November 22)

Scorpios are dauntless and secretive persons of strong feelings and determination. Often metaphysicians or occult psychologists, they are magnetic and forceful. Their desires for gratification should become urges for transmutation, spiritual growth, investigation, and insight. Given to love temptations, Scorpios should avoid painful scenes or explosive emotions and try to "cool off" quickly.

SAGITTARIUS (November 23 - December 22)

Sagittarians are devoted to noble ideals and have philosophical, intuitive minds desiring to achieve world communication. They are true disciples of the Divine Father, Teachers, and philanthropists. Travel is good for their health and spirit.

CAPRICORN (December 23 - January 20)

Capricorns are conservative, practical, and cautious, and harbor deep feelings about spiritual concepts. They desire usefulness in Cosmic Service and they organize and work for fulfillment with steady and enduring patience.

AQUARIUS (January 21 - February 19)

Aquarians are inventive and artistic. Altruists and innovators ahead of their times, they seek new ways of action, ways to move gradually from the old and established order to the long-awaited Aquarian Age.

PISCES (February 20 - March 20)

Pisceans sacrifice for a cause or for family. They are also abstract thinkers and Mystics, introspective and exclusive, understanding and sympathetic to all. Emotional and impressionable, Pisceans should learn to evolve passion into compassion.

Twenty

The
Cusps

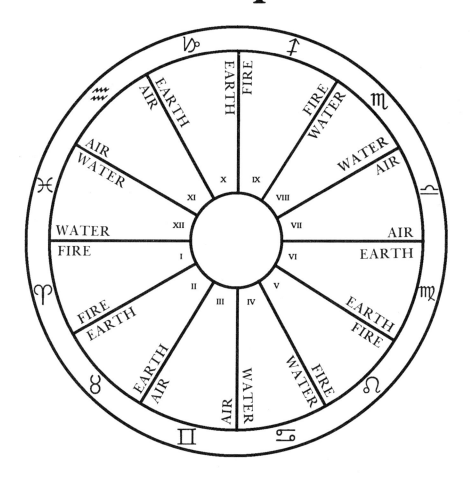

A person born during the three-degree period before or after the change of Sign partakes of the attributes of both signs. For example, if you are born when the Sun is 27 degrees of Aries, or any time up until 3 degrees of Taurus, then you are said to be born on "The Cusp" of ARIES-TAURUS, and you are characterized by both Signs.

If you are born on the Cusp, you are in a transition stage. The lesson of a previous Sign is nearly complete, but may need to be rounded out at another opportunity, or in an "interim" incarnation. Sometimes the following Sign element can to some extent be used to blend the lessons of both elements. Although these combinations are complicated, it is often a help to have a cusp personality for it gives versatility and competence.

The FIRE Sign ARIES joins the EARTH Sign TAURUS - here the self meets the desire nature and one feels the urge to go out and find success in the world of competition. Clearheaded, yet determined.

The EARTH Sign TAURUS joins the AIR Sign GEMINI - this cusp-born shows the urge to succeed being fed by the mental power of the conscious mind. Communication becomes important.

The AIR Sign GEMINI joins the WATER Sign CANCER -this six-degree span joins the field of communications with the field of the emotions, bestowing a high level of imagination.

The WATER Sign CANCER joins the FIRE Sign LEO - this cusp is vapory, giving a steamy, explosive temperament. Power, force, resourcefulness, and well-directed pressure are the qualities of the Cancer-Leo cusp born.

The FIRE Sign LEO joins the EARTH Sign VIRGO -this cusp area develops intellectual giants and fearless critics. Leaders, teachers, analysts, and demonstrators are often members of this six-degree span.

The EARTH Sign VIRGO joins the AIR Sign LIBRA -this combination makes for independence, watchfulness, and common sense, combined with the brilliant artist whose designs are beautiful and stylish. Truth and justice go hand in hand.

The AIR Sign LIBRA joins the WATER Sign SCORPIO - this is a combination of the serenity of AIR with the turbulence of WATER. Those born during this interval can travel far and fast, and develop extraordinary power and resourcefulness in overcoming obstacles. A most powerful cusp.

The WATER Sign SCORPIO joins the FIRE Sign SAGITTARIUS -this combination produces creative gifts, sparkling humor, and sincere faith. This is a combination of doers.

The FIRE Sign SAGITTARIUS joins the EARTH Sign CAPRICORN -this cusp group has supreme skill in getting above and beyond limitations. There is plenty of endurance here, producing fame, honor, and esteem.

The EARTH Sign CAPRICORN joins the AIR Sign AQUARIUS -this group desires to avoid restraint, yet remain a part of the world's business. Inventors, scientists, and psychologists come from this six-degree cusp span.

The AIR Sign AQUARIUS joins the WATER Sign PISCES -this cusp carries an active imagination, bringing gifted impressionists. Singers, actors, musicians, and authors come from this six-degree area.

The WATER Sign PISCES joins the FIRE Sign ARIES -in this group winter and spring touch, symbolizing enduring age and recurrent youth. Here is the consciousness of wisdom and the challenge of the unknown. Rashness and reserve meet; ambition overlaps dreaminess. Some of the wisest and most productive people come from this cusp.

Twenty-One

The Planets

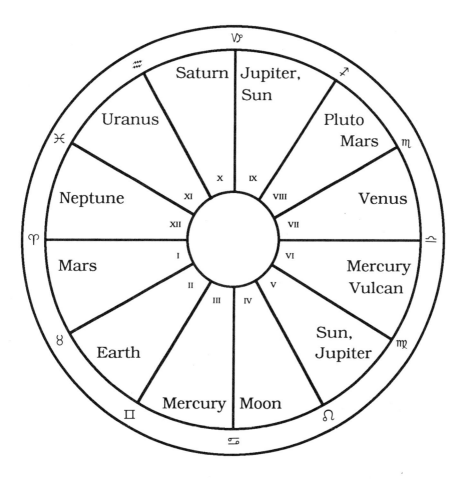

Planets focus the energies which vibrate through the world of matter. Vibration is sound and sound is creative, and thus produces various attributes in man. These vibrations - and accompanying attributes - increase in proportion to our obedience to God's Laws.

Each Planet has a distinctive tone and rate of vibration; consequently, vibrations reaching us from each Planet have particular characteristic effects. Planets are thus believed to "rule" certain aspects of our personalities. They were named for Gods in Roman Mythology and their influence on our lives reflects characteristics of those Gods. Mars, for instance, was the Roman God of war; the planet Mars vibrates as aggressiveness or combativeness, and with dynamic energy seeks to impose its own will.

For physical experiences, look to Mercury, Venus, Mars, Jupiter, and Saturn; all are a part of the environmental and mental forces, and reflect attitudes and attributes as their Mythological names indicate.

The SUN represents the vital Life-Power, will, pride, dignity, nobility, and celestial qualities. It is the "Star of the show," but may miss details.

The MOON represents the soul qualities, the emotional sensitivities, receptivity, and your personality. Your moods rise and fall and change even as the tides of the oceans ebb and flow.

MERCURY rules the reasoning mind; it observes and records, compares and relates. People ruled by MERCURY are talkative and adaptable. The conscious mind easily turns to thought and study. Its mission is to bring Light into our minds. minds

VENUS is the planet of art and rhythm, beauty, ease, and harmony. VENUS rules over love, marriage, and the family. It provides peace, poise, and tact, tenderness and gentleness, and the ability to make friends. VENUS seeks pleasure, luxury, and contentment.

MARS represents the Force that brings achievement. It is the essence of driving action, abrupt, ardent, and bold. It governs war, fevers, and fire, and the military, armaments, and iron and steel.

JUPITER is called the "Great Benefic" and brings good fortune and abundance. Jupiter governs philosophy, religion, and idealism, and also stands for humor, fun, and jollity. JUPITER can be a lawyer or judge, honorable, just, and wise.

JUPITER also sometimes indicates Cosmic Travel.

SATURN is the serious teacher and the "balance wheel" of the Zodiac. It is patient, cautious, orderly, steadfast, and disciplined. An ambitious student proud of success, SATURN learns humility by the pain of a "fall." SATURN can also experience crystallization after applying valued judgment.

URANUS is a higher octave of Mercury and frees us from false beliefs and out-worn forms. It promotes invention and discovery and gives insight, originality, and illumination. Its uniqueness often produces genius, while its instant, limitless action awakens altruism within, or may instead become unpredictable, unconventional, and surprising in general behavior. In the coming Golden Age of Harmonic Convergence, Uranus, also called the "awakener," will stimulate a questing consciousness which will open new vistas in our relationships to the Cosmic environment.

NEPTUNE is a higher octave of Venus and relates to Divine Love (Agape), the Love with a Christ-like nature. NEPTUNE is mystic, dreamy, illusive, idealistic, and prone to fantasy. At the mundane level, NEPTUNE is meditative, foggy, and visionary. It governs all liquids, medicines, drugs, and tides of the ocean.

PLUTO is an upper octave of Mars. Sometimes a destroyer, sometimes a redeemer, it could be a negative condition which can be eliminated as a better structure is envisioned. PLUTO brings change, mutation, or regeneration by its intensive, smashing revolutionary action.

VULCAN stands for selfless service. In Mythology Vulcan was an artisan in metals who tended the twenty forges which kept the heavenly spark of consciousness forever burning. VULCAN's nature is fiery, even combustible, if in close conjunction to other Planets. It is a Planet of extremes, according to position and aspects, and can be very good or very bad.

The **EARTH** is a Planet of "common sense," of conventional conduct, of "earthiness." One stays, or is pulled "down to earth," if one acts eccentrically. EARTH thus keeps us on an "even keel."

Planetary Summary

The **SUN,** the commanding note of its Planetary system, sets the "tone" into the soul-center.

The **MOON** produces the quality of a lullaby in tone.

The **VENUS** tone is keyed to beauty.

The **MERCURY** tone gives quickness and mental energy, stimulates thinking, and wants others to think equally quickly.

The **MARS** tone is stringent and forceful and gives energy, action, and enthusiasm when relating to other Planets.

The **JUPITER** tone gives generosity and humor.

The **SATURN** tone makes us serious, somber, and dutiful, and also treats of history, memory, and death.

The **URANUS** tone is like the lightening flash: unexpected, surprising, and unpredictable.

The **NEPTUNE** tone suggests Utopia and produces ingenuity, psychic tendencies, and the unknown.

The **PLUTO** tone gives subtlety.

SYMBOLS OF SIGNS AND PLANETS			
♈ Aries	♎ Libra	☉ Sun	♄ Saturn
♉ Taurus	♏ Scorpio	☽ Moon	♅ Uranus
♊ Gemini	♐ Sagittarius	☿ Mercury	♆ Neptune
♋ Cancer	♑ Capricorn	♀ Venus	♇ Pluto
♌ Leo	♒ Aquarius	♂ Mars	☊ North Node
♍ Virgo	♓ Pisces	♃ Jupiter	☋ South Node
		⊗ Part of Fortune	

Twenty-Two

The Houses

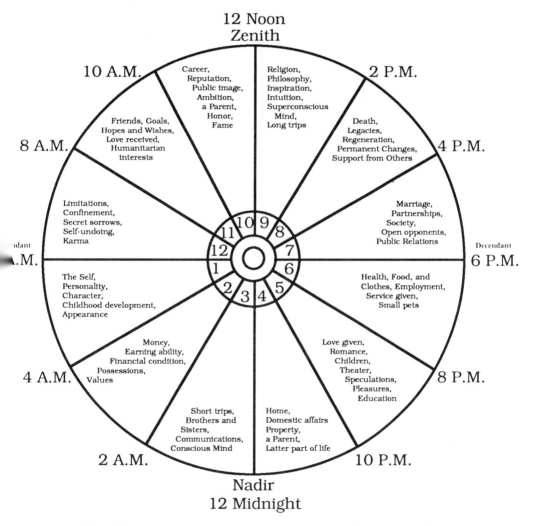

12 Noon
Zenith

10 A.M.

Career,
Reputation,
Public image,
Ambition,
a Parent,
Honor,
Fame

Religion,
Philosophy,
Inspiration,
Intuition,
Superconscious
Mind,
Long trips

2 P.M.

Friends, Goals,
Hopes and Wishes,
Love received,
Humanitarian
interests

Death,
Legacies,
Regeneration,
Permanent Changes,
Support from Others

8 A.M.

4 P.M.

Limitations,
Confinement,
Secret sorrows,
Self-undoing,
Karma

Marriage,
Partnerships,
Society,
Open opponents,
Public Relations

ıdant

Decendant

.M.

6 P.M.

The Self,
Personality,
Character,
Childhood development,
Appearance

Health, Food, and
Clothes, Employment,
Service given,
Small pets

Money,
Earning ability,
Financial condition,
Possessions,
Values

Love given,
Romance,
Children,
Theater,
Speculations,
Pleasures,
Education

4 A.M.

8 P.M.

Short trips,
Brothers and
Sisters,
Communications,
Conscious Mind

Home,
Domestic affairs
Property,
a Parent,
Latter part of life

2 A.M.

10 P.M.

Nadir
12 Midnight

The Horoscope is represented by a 360-degree wheel divided into twelve sections of thirty degrees each. These sections are called Houses, each has a symbolic meaning and governs a particular group of facets of our lives. These facets are interpreted in the Horoscope through the Planets, by their placement in the Houses, and by their Aspects.

The Houses reveal both mundane and spiritual sides to one's Horoscope. The Horoscope expresses the body in a twofold way: indirectly by the Signs on their cusps and directly by the House governorships; both work together as the Aspects and indications allow. Aspects in the First, Second, Third, Fifth, Sixth, Seventh, Tenth, and Eleventh Houses give practical, active ways of interpretation.

As the body or ego-self develops more selective moral tendencies, the influence of the Planets express themselves through the Houses on higher planes than the physical. This is especially so in the Fourth, Eighth, and Twelfth Houses which can be interpreted as karmic or occult Houses. The Fourth, Eighth, Ninth, and Twelfth Houses show inward searching for realities through chiefly Spiritual interests. In particular, Aspects within the Fourth and Twelfth Houses indicate retirement from mundane activity in order to concentrate on pursuit of the Spiritual Nature.

The First House lies under the Ascendant or Eastern Horizon and governs the moment of birth. It determines the character or personality of the individual and the real ego, the self, the "I AM," the Head.

The Second House is that of finances, earning capacity, gain or loss of movable possessions, money, or material desire.

The Third House concerns conscious mind, thought, mental ability, studies, and communications; neighbors and relatives; short trips.

The Fourth House deals with home and domestic affairs, parents, the "Universal Mother," lands, estates, mines, savings, and conditions toward the end of life.

The Fifth House is the House of children; education; romance, the love principle, the heart, and compassion; the pulpit, the theatre, or the stage; and speculation, the stock market, and games of gambling.

The Sixth House focuses in service, employment, labor, servants, and working conditions; health, hygiene, food, and clothes; and small pets.

The Seventh House treats of marriage and partnerships; all other people, social life, and the public; and contracts, law suits, and justice.

The Eighth House governs death; permanent changes; generation, de-generation, or regeneration; sex; and wills, legacies, and other people's money. The Eighth House cusp concerns karmic inheritance, for whatever had been learned in past lives, - whether material, mental, or spiritual -is revealed in the Eighth House.

The Ninth House is that of philosophy, religion, the Higher Mind, intuition, idealism, dreams, visions, and inspiration.

The Tenth House focuses on career, profession, reputation, honor, public image, worldly power and fame, moral standards, ambition, and steadfastness.

The Eleventh House is the House of altruism, friends, goals, hopes and wishes, help through influential people, humanitarian attitudes, and universal brotherhood.

The Twelfth House is the most critical one of all. It is a House of trial and limitations, a House of secret sorrows and suffering. It relates to prisons, hospitals, and other places of confinement. It can be a House of self-undoing, where one is one's own worst enemy. Through its ruler Neptune, it also concerns music, rhythm, and poetry.

THE DECANATES

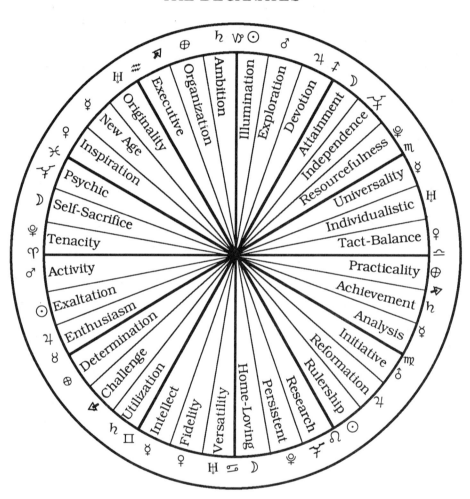

Twenty-Three

The Decanates

Key Words of the Decanates

A Decanate (Decan) is a subdivision of a Sign into three ten-degree arcs. The first Decan of a Sign is its natural ruler; the other two decans are associated with the rulers of the other two Signs of the same element (trinity).

ARIES

0°-10° Activity, Divine Fire, Zeal,
  leadership, pioneer spirit.
10°-10° Persistent ambition for power,
  noble thoughts. Affectionate, more
  head than heart.
20°-30° The heroes, power to destroy evil.

TAURUS

0°-10° Earthy, timidity, wants financial
  security, fixity of purpose.
10°-20° Discrimination, analytical, natural
  healing ability.
20°-30° Dutiful, engineer, architect,
  acriculturist.

GEMINI

0°-10° Mental ability, judge of beauty,
  experience, keen, alert, explorer.
10°-20° Captivating, versatile, sentimental,
  teacher, banker.
20°-30° Creative, visionary, advertising,
  promoter, clever, adventuresome,
  energetic.

CANCER

0°-10° Refined, industrious, dignified, psychic, home-
    maker.
10°-20° Initiative, producer, strong,
    scientific, destroyer of waste,
    eliminates old worn-out habits,
    promotes newness.
20°-30° Ideal statesman, talkative, kind,
    spiritual.

LEO

0°-10° Pride, aggressive, cheerful, hopeful,
    steadfast.
10°-20° Good natured, happy, friendly,
    benevolent.
20°-30° Extravagant, showy, liberty loving,
    out-going.

VIRGO

0°-10° Attention to details, practical,
    thorough, ethical, conscientious,
    thrifty.
10°-20° Martyr for a cause, resourceful, steady
    worker.
20°-30° Frugal, truthful, humility, faithful,
    conformist, model.

LIBRA

0°-10° Diplomatic, tactful, good judge of values, the arts.
10°-20° Original, creative, New Age worker, intuitive.
20°-30° Intellectual expertise, clever, versatile, musical
    ability.

SCORPIO

0°-10° Resourceful, secretive, decisive, endurance,
    potent.
10°-20° Psychic, occultist, spiritual, zealous, illusive.
20°-30° Testing, putting forth effort, meditative, silent.

SAGITTARIUS

0°-10° Fond of travel physically, mentally, or
    spiritually; frank and easy-going.
10°-20° Can rise to power, search out facts, rebels against
    restriction.
20°-30° Royal attitude, teacher of philosophy-
    metaphysics.

CAPRICORN

0°-10° Forerunner for better conditions, good business
    judgment, ambitious for success.
10°-20° Manager, organizer, executive type, large
    enterprises.
20°-30° Universal progression, can scale the heights in any
    endeavor.

AQUARIUS

0°-10° Progressive, follows own ideals, inventive.
10°-20° Convincing talker, mental acumen, contacts inner
    planes.
20°-30° Imaginative, inspirational, inventive, creative.

PISCES

0°-10° Mystic, strong love nature, esoteric seer, seeks
    wisdom.
10°-20° Helps others, changeable feelings, moody, likes
    variety.
20°-30° Eventful lives, dual careers, adaptable, can contact
    astral or higher planes. Passion to compassion.

Twenty-Four

The Elements

The twelve Signs of the Zodiac are divided into Trinities of the four Elements FIRE, EARTH, AIR, and WATER. FIRE and AIR are positive in nature; EARTH and WATER Signs are negative. The FIRE Trinity consists of Aries, Leo, and Sagittarius; the EARTH Trinity of Taurus, Virgo, and Capricorn; the AIR Trinity of Gemini, Libra, and Aquarius; and the WATER Trinity of Cancer, Scorpio, and Pisces.

These Elements are not of chemical composition, but are rather symbolic subdivisions of matter. FIRE symbolizes energy which moves in a spiral; thus, any center of force controlled by fire can be seen as whirling vortex or wheel. EARTH is the symbolic virgin element, the natural matrix. AIR stands for that which permits the circulation of all substances (for example, without air, fire would be dormant). And WATER represents the "seed" of all things, the Pearl of Great Price, the secret vitality of humanity (for humanity is a "seed" of God).[1]

The Elements can indicate personality characteristics of people born under their Trinities. For example, they can show how one manifests and harnesses the vast amounts of Cosmic Energy available to us. FIRE, the exhilarating energy of real health, adds great amounts of physical vitality to one's whole system. EARTH brings home a positive attitude to help one take circumstances in stride and to aid one in putting vitality to practical work and purpose. AIR circulates vitality and focuses energy, helping one relax and thus manage the stress of modern life. WATER acts as the energy and emotion of self-awareness and helps one attain wisdom and serenity.

The Elements also indicate the type of lesson we must work out in our present incarnation. Those born under the FIRE Trinity are meant to respond to Spiritual Love and compassion; those under the EARTH Trinity are born to learn and practice service to humanity; those under the AIR Trinity must learn cooperation and brotherhood; and those born under the WATER Trinity must work toward peace and harmony. People born under the "Cusps" of Signs have lessons blending those of the two Elements.

Fire

FIRE is an Element of drive and ambition, sometimes needing control, and FIRE Signs represent energy and enthusiasm. They also represent the first streaming forth of Divine energy to be under concentrated use for advancement. They are spiritual, philosophic, energetic, forceful, active, idealistic, and temperamental. FIRE Signs are most powerful when in the First, Fifth, and Ninth Houses of your Chart, and next powerful when a majority of planets are placed therein. If the SUN is in a FIRE Sign, its power is increased by the congenial Element. The FIRE Signs are ARIES (independent), LEO (self-motivating), and SAGITTARIUS (future—oriented).

ARIES, the first FIRE Sign, is the fire of the head, the untamed fire of impulse, ardor, and emotion, the fire which illumines and gives Light, which purifies the fiery quality of the Will. ARIES is most pronounced because it is the Cardinal Sign. It is pioneering and impulsive, concerned with body consciousness and well-being. If negative, the ARIES fire is angry, and gives off great heat. The smouldering flames may break forth in a quick combustion.

LEO represents the fire of the heart, the steadily controlled fire of affection. It is strong because it is the Fixed Sign of the group. It awakens the Spiritual Will. It is executive and loyal, creative, magnetic, and sometimes definitely forceful. The emphasis is on independence, radiation, ideals, and a sense of justice. In LEO the flame is golden and luminous; it burns steadily so that all may benefit from its warmth and light. LEO teaches the lesson of Love. Souls striving to master this Element will have many experiences demonstrating completely the true meaning of Love. Love must be handled with wisdom or it may result in loss and unhappiness. Use insight, intuition, and desire for justice for solutions of problems of self.

SAGITTARIUS is the Mutable Sign of the FIRE group. It stands for power of distribution. SAGITTARIANS are brilliant, jovial, and philosophical, often with flashes of inspiration. SAGITTARIANS have keen wit, which in many instances evolves into the gift of prophecy.

Earth

EARTH represents the practical, sensible, and reliable qualities of consciousness in the field of physical evolution and serves as a probation place for its inhabitants. We residents of EARTH receive and respond to the penetrating waves of vibration influenced primarily by the SUN and the MOON. EARTH Signs are most powerful when in the Second, Sixth, and Tenth Houses, or when a majority of Planets are placed therein. The EARTH Signs are TAURUS (systematic and steadfast), VIRGO (conservative), and CAPRICORN (materialistic).

TAURUS is the Fixed Sign of the EARTH Element representing the broad plains of the Planet. It stands for those who follow routine with endless patience with the will to build slowly and carefully and for long-lasting endurance. They work for solid accomplishment and hold firmly to their steadfast will to attain their purpose and to achieve real, tangible results. Their character is "matter-of-fact" in the constructive sense, rendering it stable and determined in its on-going progress. Things of enduring value are produced, and because Taurians are endowed with a strong Will, they are able to make long-range plans for future ennobling.

VIRGO is the Mutable Sign of the EARTH Element. It represents the deep valleys of our Planet. The VIRGO intellect is efficient and analytical, concerned with work and service. It gives its attention to fine details whether the project is large or small. VIRGO desires to serve as a humble worker, for the needs of others inspires their careful and efficient, sometimes meticulous, attention and effort to earn respect for their assistance. They inwardly sense discrimination between essentially valuable things and those of little worth. VIRGO is also much concerned with physical health and well-being.

CAPRICORN is the Cardinal Sign of the EARTH Element and is therefore strong and pioneering in nature. It symbolizes the rugged mountains and high stone cliffs of the EARTH Planet. It is the most aggressive of the EARTH Signs, concerned with social standing and the environment. It assumes authority, responsibility, and initiative with unfailing persistence. CAPRICORN works from the standpoint of recognition, desiring to reach the "top" in status, whatever the circumstance. The Elements combining with CAPRICORN for best results would be from the WATER Signs, because they work together to nourish and replenish the EARTH.

Air

AIR is regarded as a unifier which can bring together and balance the other temperaments. The AIR Signs represent the mental and super-mental qualities and relate to the Human Kingdom. These are the knowledge gatherers; they work through the intellect and intuition. AIR Signs are most powerful when in the Third, Seventh, and Eleventh Houses, or when many Planets are placed therein. The SUN in AIR adds brilliance to the Chart. The AIR Signs are GEMINI (intellectual), LIBRA (companionable), and AQUARIUS (humanitarian).

GEMINI represents the Mutable Sign of the AIR group. It has an inquiring type of mind, is curious, and wants to know the WHY of things. It is versatile and investigative, always seeking change for betterment. GEMINI wends its way through many and varied circumstances, scattering its knowledge with expert skill, determination, and purpose. Actions seem always backed by reason and a bid for freedom.

LIBRA is the strong Cardinal Sign of the AIR Element. It is known for its pleasing personality as it works for harmony and friendly relationships. Most concerned with judgment and balance, LIBRAS seek to calm the "winds" of the great "equinoctial storms" of the Fall Season. Sociable and companionable, they avoid argument and contention by maintaining silence when "ill weather" prevails.

AQUARIUS is the Fixed Sign of the AIR Element. It represents the cold, electric, clean air of Winter. It stands for brotherhood and altruism. Much is now expected of the AQUARIAN because of the approach of the Aquarian Age, now only a few years away.[2] Although the temperament of AQUARIANS is sometimes eccentric, they demand freedom for themselves and for others. They feel absolute loyalty to their friends, and as idealistic types are intuitive, often with unusual and surprising attitudes; nevertheless they are honest and studious.

Water

The WATER Signs represent vital and emotional qualities, deep, reflective, and responsive. Because of its fluidic state, it is susceptible to impressions and the forces of E.S.P. WATER Signs are easily influenced, moody, and sympathetic, and tend toward mediumship, or contact with the "inner planes." WATER Signs are most powerful when in the Fourth, Eighth, and Twelfth Houses, or when a majority of Planets are placed therein. The SUN is least powerful in these Signs, but if the MOON is in a WATER Sign, its power is greatly increased. The WATER Signs are CANCER (tender emotions), SCORPIO (extremes), and PISCES (profound, subtle, mystic).

CANCER is the Cardinal Sign of the WATER Element, and represents water in its fluidic state. It is pioneering yet changeable and fluctuating, subject to many phases of personality. Aware and concerned with the subconscious soul qualities, it is usually patriotic and home-loving; symbolically, it is the "Cosmic Mother."

SCORPIO is the Fixed Sign of the WATER Element, and represents water in its frozen state. The highly developed SCORPIOS are ardent defenders of their faith, and stand firmly on their convictions. SCORPIO wields much power through its ruling Planets, Mars and Pluto. Keyed to investigation of the occult and spiritual forces, SCORPIOS are highly secretive and keep their ideals to themselves, unless challenged, at which time they become daring and aggressive. Water bestows placidity, but when disturbed by some other element-such as air or high wind - water may be lashed into an angry sea. The auras of SCORPIOS abound with magnetism, rendering their healing and nurturing forces tremendously effective. Romantic involvements may be explosive.

PISCES is the Mutable Sign of the WATER Element, representing water in its vaporous state (steam or fog), for here the physical verges toward the Metaphysical and is therefore elusive. To blend the energies of the Piscean Age with the emerging Aquarian Age is to change from receptive moods to out-going will-to-action.

LEVELS OF INTERPRETATION FOR THE ELEMENTS

FIRE	EARTH	AIR	WATER
Will	Common	Thought	Intuition
Intention	Material	Plan	Emotion
Idea	Fate	Theory	Creative
Divine	Action and Reaction	Intelligence	Depth of Thought

1. There is a fifth element, LIGHT, whose symbology is even more "rarified" than that of the others. LIGHT, with Love, crossed the material body with the Angelic Soul to bring forth the Celestial Being, Developed Man. One who has been "born again" of the Holy Spirit. LIGHT, being a transcendent Element, does not appear graphically in the Zodiac as do the other Elements.

2. Written 1988.

Twenty-Five

The Seasons

We are products of time and of karma. We must eventually respond to causes we put in motion at some time in the past. Because of this, the Seasons can serve as useful timing devices as we delve into the depths of the significance of the Pentacle Points. Through the Seasons, Cardinal Points (the Spring and Fall Equinoxes, and the Summer and Winter Solstices) flow many creative functions that contribute to the birth of our Higher Consciousness.

The Cardinal Points of the Natural Zodiac are most important, and each one corresponds to a Season. The ascendant point (6 a.m.) corresponds to Spring, and represents the self seeing the self. Summer is the zenith (noon), a destiny factor where we perfect our ego and gain public image. The descendant (6 p.m.) is Fall and represents the soul's seeking for companionship, and the realization of difference between ourselves and others. And the nadir (midnight) corresponds to Winter and is the beginning and end of the present cycle of life.

The Spring Equinox Point

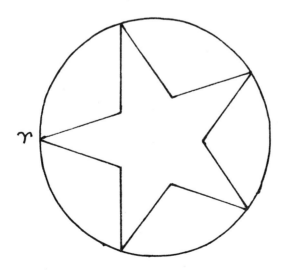

The Spring or Vernal Equinox Point starts in the Fire Sign ARIES. It is called the Astrological New Year when the SUN rises at the Spring Equinox on or about March 21st. It is like a new awakening throughout all nature, a resurrection of new growth. It gives the signal to go ahead and stands for pioneering and new starts. It presents a new perspective with its own manner of expression and suggests a better way to identify the source and quality of power for use in our research. The time is right for creative activity during this the opening month of the year. As ARIES rules the head, the part of the body receiving the greatest out-pouring of the SUN's energy, it signifies an impetus for change and for using this increased energy in positive, new ways. Something new pervades the atmosphere, something we all feel to some degree. There is a new "spring" in our very step and the time is ripe for rejuvenation and development of new talents and growth in wisdom.

The Summer Solstice Point

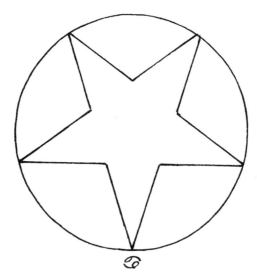

The Summer Solstice Point starts in the Water Sign CANCER. The SUN rises higher until it reaches the Zenith at the Summer Solstice, on or about June 21st of each year. "Water" relates to subconsciousness, soul qualities, and psychic ability at a level which, when purified, may express itself as Divine Love. This Point can become a test of one's attributes and emotions. The MOON, ruler of CANCER, rules the tides of the oceans, which correspond physically to one's changing moods and emotions. Control of the emotions is the first step.

Easily hurt feelings must be transmuted to forgiveness and peaceful attitudes. Tune in to your "Still-Point;" relax and meditate. Learn not to "push the river." Make an honest effort to evaluate yourself in relation to your home and to society at large. This is your own private test and need not be judged by others. Although one with a negative self-image tends to withdraw from the world, such a person really needs to build self-confidence instead. Remove any negative thoughts from your mind and suggest that your "head rule your heart" while being aware of Divine Love receptivity.

The Autumn Equinox Point

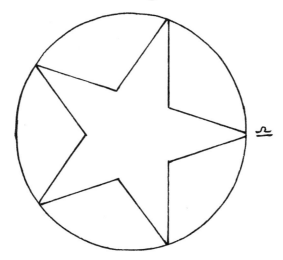

The Autumn Equinox Point starts in the Air Sign LIBRA. The SUN enters the Zodiacal point on or about September 24th. Of all Elements Air is most subtle. One must develop dispassion, a standing aside in observance of human attributes for the achievement of harmonious brotherhood in sharing with others. "Air" people are here to develop altruism and learn the lesson of Brotherhood by way of the intellect, discrimination, poise, equanimity, and balance. LIBRA natives must strive to gain equilibrium, to bring order into the life, and to stabilize a harmonious environment. Flow and rhythm of vibration bring fruition and growth through imagination, creativity, cosmic ideals, and harvesting power.

The breath may be used to stabilize and balance your forces, thus aiding in expansion, communication, E.S.P. and soul development. Your endowment of charm and grace usually wins approval from others. Above all, LIBRA promotes cooperation- you have keen insight such that your counseling ability and sense of fairness brings a sense of justice and a willingness to work together with your contemporaries.

The Winter Solstice Point

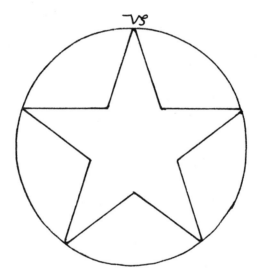

The Winter Solstice Point starts in the Earth Sign CAPRICORN. The SUN enters the Winter Solstice on or about December 21st of every year. Earth Signs are concerned with service. Those striving to master this Element will be absorbed in practical and materialistic matters, which should be turned toward the spiritual consciousness for developing efficiency. Both firmness and responsibility are needed for a higher standard of stability. CAPRICORN'S are the doers of the Earth Signs, standing for organization and a persistent drive for excellence. They forge ahead, always competing at meeting all obligations in prime time. Security is important to their way of life, and they will never let obstacles stand in the way of their climb to the top.

Growth toward consolidation of purpose may be accomplished through service to humanity in general. One who serves is on the Path of Discipleship and has gained wisdom at a high level, for it was said:

"He who gives service is the greatest of all."

-Matt. 23:11-

Twenty-Six

The
Main Aspects

In your Horoscope, Aspects describe the relationship of the planets to each other. They are determined by the distance in degrees between planets. The more exact the distance, the more powerful it will be, whether in a positive or negative way. Most Aspects are allowed a 6° orb, or sphere of influence.

Each Aspect is generally considered beneficial, malefic, or variable. This is, however, a simplification. A beneficial, or "lucky" Aspect can bring good fortune without effort, which gives the individual no incentive to strive for his or her personal development. A malefic Aspect, however, can be considered not so much a misfortune as a great challenge, an opportunity for soul growth. Thus, simple interpretations of Aspects can be very misleading. They overlook the ultimate truth around us, that of the greater order of the Universe, of a constant progression of souls. Only a careful analysis of Aspects will present us with our true potential as beings evolving toward Divinity.

Studied along with the Element, Quality, House, and Sign of the involved Planets, the Aspects can be subtle tools of great insight. For example, inharmonious facets of a "malefic" Aspect are reduced in influence when one or both of the Planets involved is in its own House or Sign.

Also, Sign and Quality can help explain how our tendencies and personalities relate to our overall soul development. Aspects in Cardinal Signs concern with debts from past lives which must be changed through action. Fixed Sign Aspects deal with deeply imbedded habits from the past which must be changed through giving up the self-will. And Mutable Sign Aspects represent characteristics just beginning to show through poor decisions and improper action, the easiest challenges to overcome.

Houses explain the nature of desirable actions that will enhance our development. Relevant Aspects and Planets in the First, Second, Third, Fifth, Seventh, Tenth, and Eleventh Houses deal with practical and active solutions of challenges. Those in the Fourth, Eighth, Ninth, and Twelfth Houses operate more inwardly in search of realities, chiefly through various psychic abilities. The Fourth and Twelfth Houses in particular indicate a retreat from mundane activity to pursue more spiritual concerns.

Many different Aspects can occur in one's Horoscope. The Main Aspects will be described here; in an earlier chapter, the less common Aspects that are particularly useful for Pentacle analysis are presented. These descriptions will be brief; numerous astrological texts are available to provide the interested reader with more extensive treatments of various Aspects. (One such good text is Robert Pelletier's *Planets in Aspects,* 1974, Gloucester, MA: Para Research.)

CONJUNCTION (0°)

This Aspect intensifies the natures of the Planets involved, bringing them prominence and power. It begins a new cycle and emphasizes energy. It may be either harmonious or malefic, depending on the Planets involved. Planets in their own Signs tend to dominate a conjunction. Allow a 5° orb.

SEXTILE (60°)

A major Aspect giving opportunity as shown in your Natal Chart. This Aspect is more effective, as it gives mental perception for bringing ideas into manifestation; however, one must act upon these quickly in order to realize their benefit. The sextile brings harmony and help for character improvement.

SQUARE (90°)

This Aspect signifies an obstacle, a struggle, or discord. It often represents problems we have failed to overcome in former lives. If the challenges of a square are worked out in the first half of life, then they can become as trines.

GRAND SQUARE

This is a series of four square Aspects that form a complete geometric square. It is a challenging configuration requiring a constructive and balanced use of energies to prevent chaos. The Quality of the Square is important. (See Chapter 27, "The Trines, Squares, and their Combinations.")

T-SQUARE

A configuration of imbalance, this is a Grand Square with one Element missing. The empty end will reveal a missing facet of one's character, a facet which must be developed during this life. When a Planet transits this empty end, one may experience a time of crisis.

TRINE (120°)

A lucky Aspect, this provides ease, harmony, strong support, and protection. These are the results of labors in past lives, rewards earned then and now effortlessly obtained.

GRAND TRINE

A group of three trines that make up an equilateral triangle, this is the most fortunate configuration. It indicates honor, success, protection, and harmony in life. The Elemental nature of the trine is important. If it is an Earth Trine, for example, one tends to be lucky and attracted to material things, which could lead to selfishness and impede spiritual growth, while if it is a Water Trine, great psychic talent is possible.

QUINCUNX/INCONJUNCT (150°)

This aspect may relate to healing and service and to regeneration of character. It may be an Aspect of mental stress, guilt, or discord, or of something that needs adjustment. It sometimes indicates Karma, especially if it occurs in the occult houses (4th, 8th, 12th). This is an Aspect of mixed blessings but can be modified to the good by right actions and attitudes and can thus lead to growth and greater maturity. It shows what we must "put up with," work around, and adapt to. Try to overcome stress by assuming balance and poise. We are stronger than we think and can adjust to circumstances. This discipline brings inner growth and blessings. Allow only a 3° orb for this Aspect.

OPPOSITION (180°)

A separative Aspect, this represents inner tension and outer struggle - forces pulling in opposite directions that cause distress and force a need for cooperation. It brings growth through an awareness of the need for discrimination, tact, diplomacy, and strategy, as well as through internal strength which can be harmonized and utilized through self-conscious effort. It is important in examining an opposition to examine the nature of the Houses involved, for the consciousness is focused chiefly there. The characteristics of the relevant Planets will also provide important insights. The Elements also contribute to our understanding of the forces in play. In a Fire and Air opposition, ideal mental harmony is often denied or can be a source of tension. In an Earth and Water opposition, emotions oppose the practical influence and a problem must be resolved between the head and the heart.

MAIN ASPECTS SUMMARY CHART

SYMBOL	NAME	ANGLE	NATURE
☌	Conjunction	0°	Power
✶	Sextile	60°	Opportunity
□	Square	90°	Obstacle
△	Trine	120°	Very Good
⚻	Quincunx	150°	Sacrifice
☍	Opposition	180°	Separative

Twenty-Seven

The Trines and Squares

Their Combinations of Elements and Qualities

The Horoscope has four possible Grand Trines, or Trinities. Each Trine joins together Signs of similar Elements; thus, we have the Fire, Earth, Air, and Water Trines. The Trines deal with instinct and with awareness of needs for food, shelter, and protection.

The three Grand Squares of the Horoscope (also called Crosses or Quadruplicities) join together Signs of the same Quality. We thus have Cardinal, Fixed, and Mutable Squares. The Squares give us insight into such matters as conscious identity, physical life, the desire for possessions, "the plain facts," reason, competition, aggressiveness, and the development of ego.

The Elements and Qualities may also be analyzed in combinations.

Three-Pointed Stars as Elements

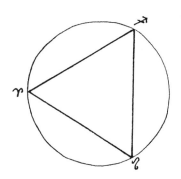

FIRE

ARIES—The Head, concentrated energy.

LEO—The Heart, Will to create, achievement, leadership.

SAGITTARIUS—Distribution of energy, mediating idealist.

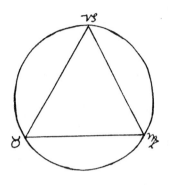

EARTH

CAPRICORN—Organization, order, ambition, executive.

TAURUS—Finances, agriculture, steadfast.

VIRGO—Selfless service, capability, humility.

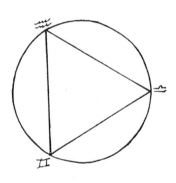

AIR

LIBRA—Balanced harmony, art, co-operation.

AQUARIUS—Originality, science, genius.

GEMINI—Intellect, communication, versatile, literary.

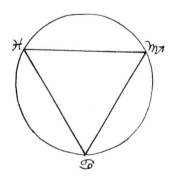

WATER

CANCER—Emotions, soul qualities.

SCORPIO—Intense desires. Will to conquer, leadership.

PISCES—Sympathetic understanding, forgiveness, vision.

The Crosses—Four-Pointed Stars

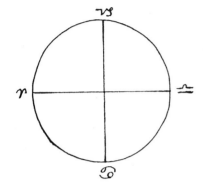

The **CARDINAL CROSS** is on the angles, and is thus angular and strong. It represents the Pioneers of the Horoscope and areas from which adjustments must be made, although one may require great effort to overcome the problems.

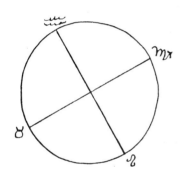

The **FIXED CROSS** represents the Perfectors, who must take on the most stubborn circumstances and, with tremendous effort, work to stamp out fixed tendencies. Negative habits of long standing need to be overcome.

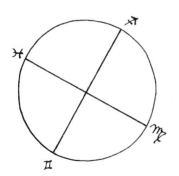

The **MUTABLE CROSS** represents the Developers, who try to adjust and cooperate to overcome their difficulties. Many times a misuse of free will has been the problem. To adopt a program of "Thy Will be done—Thy Will, not mine" would help the limiting situations.

The Squares—Four-Pointed Stars

CARDINAL SQUARE—Activity, Crises

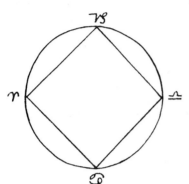

ARIES—Wants freedom to be.

CANCER—Wants to belong, to be protected.

LIBRA—Wants to be equal, balanced.

CAPICORN—Wants to be responsible, to organize.

FIXED SQUARE—Values

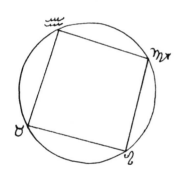

TAURUS—Wants to indulge, appetites.

LEO—Wants self-expansion, willful.

SCORPIO—Wants control, permanent changes.

AQUARIUS—Wants wisdom, dominion.

MUTABLE SQUARE—Relationships

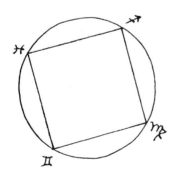

GEMINI—Wants to know.

VIRGO—Wants to be thorough.

SAGITTARIUS—Wants to explore the Infinite.

PISCES—Wants the Ultimate, God realization.

Combinations of Elements and Qualities

CARDINAL - FIRE

This combination has a high-spirited, energetic nature and much independence in thought and action. It has enthusiasm, keen understanding, great skill and ability for success, flashes of genius, and talent. It can also tend toward selfishness and egoism. It is ambitious for recognition and works for a professional career.

CARDINAL - EARTH

Practical and ambitious, people with this combination desire material advancement. They are reserved, prudent, systematic, cautious, tactful, and diplomatic in conduct. They are well organized, have good financial ability, and use valued judgment in ways of living and working.

CARDINAL - AIR

This is a combination of great refinement, honor, and noble aims. These people are courteous and cultured, socially successful, appreciative of the beautiful, intuitive, capable, and diligent. Lawyers, architects, orators, and politicians appear in this group.

CARDINAL - WATER

People in this combination have strong and romantic personalities and are sensitive and sympathetic, affectionate and demonstrative, and somewhat changeable. They tend to have psychic impressions and are very intuitive.

FIXED - FIRE

This is a combination of strong will, magnetism, and energy producing success in life. It also denotes great persistence, pride, fidelity, and practical determination, and favors employment in government or science.

FIXED - EARTH

This combination usually denotes a very materialistic mind, determined and persistent and sometimes over-confident, opinionated, slow, and over-cautious. Patience here wins over problem-solving and limitations disappear. People with this combination tend toward real-estate, mining, or agriculture.

FIXED - AIR

This combination gives dignity, refinement, and trustworthiness. Reserved and stable in manner, those with this combination are aristocratic and elegant and live conventionally with attention to society and the elite. They often pursue artistic work, such as sculpting or painting in oils.

FIXED - WATER

People with this combination are strong, silent, and unexpressive of emotions, although extreme in their feelings, whether love or hate. But those feelings are not easily aroused, and much emotion remains latent. Many temptations come into the lives of those in this group; thus, they require a great deal of moral courage. They have receptive and psychic natures and favor mercantile or governmental occupations.

MUTABLE - FIRE

This combination gives ardent feelings and a very independent and keen temperament. It brings an eventful career and many unusual experiences, and favors religious tendencies. Much talent or even genius develops under these attributes. They may sometimes be eccentric.

MUTABLE - EARTH

Those with this combination have a critical, analytical mind and tend to be methodical and thorough. Life may become too formal or monotonous for them, but they should try to avoid fear and hesitation when opportunities appear. They tend toward unglamorous careers such as shop-keeping, plumbing,or carpenter work.

MUTABLE - AIR

This is a combination of keen intellectual ability and refined personality, with a possibility to develop in either scientific or literary fields. This combination also tends toward accounting, secretarial, or teaching professions. Much depends on the environment for best expression here.

MUTABLE - WATER

This combination denotes a susceptible, easily influenced disposition, and is more favorable for females than males. If Planets are favorably placed and aspected, a good position in life is attainable. People with this combination should be ready to take an opportunity when offered - to dare to grow. They have abilities in nursing, cooking, nutrition, and sales.

Twenty-Eight

The Pentads

When a Horoscope is interpreted by readings of the Planets in Signs and Houses and by the Planetary Aspects only, we intuit that there must be something more. It may be in regard to areas not occupied by any Planet or Occult Point. Often the House cusp rulership will indicate something of importance in an area that could have been overlooked.

Every one of the 360 degrees of the Zodiac has a symbolic meaning. The Ascendant, Descendant, Mid-Heaven (Zenith), and Nadir offer further information, even if not occupied by a Planet or relating to their important Aspects. The positions of the Nodes give further characteristic details and sometimes the Fixed Stars point to gleanings accrued by their positions in Sign, House, and Aspect.

The Science of Astrology postulates that there are no absolutely pure effects, although each Aspect is an important part of the Horoscope Chart as a whole and may be useful for various clarifications.

In applying the Pentad Degree Readings, Planets occupying an exact degree with the Pentad Degree signify a strengthening of that area of the Horoscope, by Sign and House. To determine the power of Pentad Aspects, consider one degree either side of the exact degree as being next in strength, if the Planet is mid-way, draw from the nearest degree.

We must have a 0° Point and we must have a 30° Point. They seem to be one and the same, but the degree and minutes will point to the greater strengths. In *any* case this will act as a "Cusp" position in which the powers of both are imminent and active.

A Pentad represents a group of "five" - a potential of etheric and celestial radiance of growth and vitality within us. The Pentad general characteristics are:

0 Degrees		A neophyte in the Sign.
5	″	An evolving, developing process.
10	″	Unfolding and exploring.
15	″	Investigation.
20	″	Diligence, searching, analysis.
25	″	Beginning change in quality.
30	″	Desire for further outreach.

The Penta-Rhythms are teleological - they go forward eternally, but if negative, they are rapidly regressive. Action follows MEDITATION; thus, the "God-seed" within will move toward a goal.

The Pentads of ARIES

0 Degrees		The path is open; walk with joy in the Light.
5	"	Enter the glory of the soul-path and rejoice.
10	"	Seek and find your Star of Destiny.
15	"	Meditate on points of revealment.
20	"	Learn the rules and work with diligence.
25	"	Let the soul reign over the senses.
30	"	My soul must turn to God for wisdom.

The Pentads of TAURUS

0 Degrees		A degree of Planning.
5	"	The soul is a Cosmic vehicle on an eternal journey.
10	"	The "call" to illumination.
15	"	Be alert, hear the "inner voice."
20	"	Trust and try for Eternity is *now*.
25	"	Born to be purposeful, fruitful, and forgiving.
30	"	Emerging potentials.

The Pentads of GEMINI

0 Degrees		Define and refine and accept the findings.
5	"	Use vision and insight for a forward look to the future.
10	"	Change to positive and dynamic ways of life.
15	"	Resonance has made its impact on mind and heart.
20	"	One's best friend is the God within; therefore, be true to yourself.
25	"	See thoughts intuit new tasks.
30	"	Accept His Will and its Divine order and plan.

The Pentads of CANCER

0 Degrees		My eyes look Star-ward.
5	"	Awake with joyful vision - that which inspires is Eternal.
10	"	The water of life is flowing, merging, and purifying my world.
15	"	A time to turn to the Spiritual Light.
20	"	Become a peace mediator for God.
25	"	A time to center the life in the presence of Universal Love.
30	"	Soul opening to great ideals.

The Pentads of LEO

0 Degrees		God's Will be done in me.
5	"	Develop loving attitudes and sincerity of heart.
10	"	Show the forces of Love and Light for all to see.
15	"	Work and pray with an expectant heart.
20	"	Discard the ego and show humility.
25	"	Surrender to the Will and Wisdom of God.
30	"	Love is the fulfilling of the Law.

The Pentads of VIRGO

0 Degrees		Lord of Love, let me be ready to serve.
5	"	Visualize a "spiral" and start climbing.
10	"	Work for harmony, beauty, and Love.
15	"	Through God's Will I receive quickening, inspiration, and revelation.
20	"	His mighty plan correlates to the vibrations of the Universal Pulse.
25	"	Cling to the upward spiral growth pattern.
30	"	Be tranquil and quiet; Peace-be still.

The Pentads of LIBRA

0 Degrees Learn from the past, work in the present, and build for the future.
5   "   Rise from body to soul by conscious awareness.
10   "   Knowledge alone does not result in soul-growth.
15   "   Stars guide your journey.
20   "   Follow your celestial Star-Points.
25   "   Develop new responses and choose the better way for all concerned.
30   "   With dedicated effort, victory is assured.

The Pentads of SCORPIO

0 Degrees Divine Order is at work in your life.
5   "   Do all things in dignity and in Order.
10   "   A degree for Spiritual Development.
15   "   Each constellation contributes to your spiritual growth.
20   "   To deny the influence of the stars is to deny the wisdom of your higher self.
25   "   The Spirit in you gives you understanding.
30   "   Set a good example in speech, conduct, faith, and love.

The Pentads of SAGITTARIUS

0 Degrees Let the soul free itself.
5   "   Become ONE with Infinite Spirit.
10   "   A key to transcend time and space.
15   "   Build your bridge from the mundane to the Spiritual.
20   "   Decide between the profits and the prophets.
25   "   Join with the Cosmic patterns in your chart and attain your goal.
30   "   Time to transcend aloft and live Universally.

The Pentads of CAPRICORN

0 Degrees The need to be real and to know your realness.
5   ″   The need for faith, good-will, and devotion.
10   ″   The time to take the "mist" out of Mystery.
15   ″   To set our "wills" with the Will-of-God that
             we may fulfill the Divine Plan.
20   ″   Let inspiration prevail.
25   ″   Behold, I make all things new.
30   ″   Be a beacon of Light, Love, and Wisdom.

The Pentads of AQUARIUS

0 Degrees Be comforted, strengthened and enlightened.
5   ″   A refinement of intellect.
10   ″   An idealist about Love; may prefer platonic
             friendships.
15   ″   Creative and inventive; higher achievers.
20   ″   Resonance with the "serpent-power."
25   ″   Judging one's alternatives - sole or soul; choose
             either the selfish and solitary Sole-Self or
             the sharing expanding Soul-Self.
30   ″   To know that God is Love unifies all
             philosophies.

The Pentads of PISCES

0 Degrees This "Path" brings the realization of "Grace."
5   ″   Express detachment from the "glamours" of
             the Earth.
10   ″   Progress on the Path to a higher octave of
             development.
15   ″   Seek the brilliance of the shining Sun.
20   ″   The realization of Divine purpose and goal.
25   ″   Be ye transformed by the renewing of your
             mind.
30   ″   "Ye are Gods; and all are the children of the
             Most High." Psalm 82:6.

Gods!?
If not now - surely "in the making."

Twenty-Nine

The
Fixed Stars

Fixed Stars vibrate to sensitive points in our birth charts with influence felt mostly by conjunction with a Natal Planet point. The Fixed Stars have yet to be explored in depth, although greater attention to them is now apparent in new books and magazine articles. Now that we have a way of analyzing our Pentacle Points, we have an even greater opportunity to utilize the Fixed Stars in our Horoscopes. These Points of Living Light will thus prove increasingly helpful to our awakening.

We will consider only Stars of the greater vibrational importance. Many books treat these Stars more comprehensively; this brief list should merely serve to spark interest in further research.

The movement of the Fixed Stars is estimated to be about fifty seconds a year. Degree positions given are approximate. Allow a six degree orb for aspects.

IN ARIES

Andromeda	14°	Considered fortunate, bestows honor.
Mirach	29°	Good cheer, prosperity, art.

IN TAURUS

Algol	25°	Considered unfortunate.
Alcyon (Pleiades)	29°	Ambition.

IN GEMINI

Aldebaran	9°	Energetic, martial.
Rigel	16°	Benevolent, fame.
Betelgeuse	28°	Ingenuity, riches.

IN CANCER

Sirius 14° A brilliant star of *Love and Wisdom,* it develops understanding and heightens Spiritual awareness. Gives the ability to break through to other Solar Systems and to higher evolution; as it gives out a vast amount of heat and light energy, one may find further unfoldment. *Love* is neither emotion nor sentiment, but that which determines to work for Unity and wholeness; *Wisdom* is a blend of intuition and insight which opens the way to Spiritual Perception into new possibilities. Signifies wealth and fortune.

Procyon 25° An influence like that of the Moon and Mars.

IN LEO

Regulus 29° Variable, like Jupiter and Mars.

IN VIRGO

Denebola 20° Like Mercury.

IN LIBRA

Spica 23° Wealth, beauty, art.
Arcturus 23° Fortunate, fame, honor.

IN SCORPIO

Alphecca 11° Fortunate, personal magnetism, healing.

IN SAGITTARIUS

Antares 9° A red giant star, headstrong like Mars.

IN CAPRICORN

Vega   14° Enterprising, a leader.

IN AQUARIUS

Altair   0° Confident, courageous, diplomatic.
(the Eagle)

IN PISCES

Formalhaut   3° Fortunate like Jupiter and Venus,
                       inheritance.
Deneb   5° Northern Cross.
Markab   22° Uncertain like Venus and Mars,
                       eminence.

Conclusion

Interest in metaphysics is universal. We instinctively seek something beyond the mundane. As we strive to find a better way of life, a basic urge - something buried deep in our subconscious mind - motivates us to consider our spiritual possibilities. To study the esoteric sciences is to cultivate those possibilities. In esoteric astrology, we learn of the powerful influence of the energies that emanate from the planets and our zodiacal group as well as from the many other stars in our galaxy. We also learn that we should employ these powers constructively.

This book has touched on a whole panorama of challenges to be met, strengths to be developed, and arts to be mastered - of "Points to be polished" during the Soul's Journey through the Earth Plane. The combined efforts of our conscious subconscious and superconscious minds can effect such polishing when they focus on the hope of growth approaching transcendence. We may thus become more than we presently are through our hope for growth and our innate will-to-good and through an increased study of metaphysical material. These endeavors will confirm and stimulate our higher nature.

The study of our Stars of Destiny can help us to align ourselves with that higher nature and to cultivate our aims enthusiastically within the Age of Harmonic Mutation. When we have constructed our own Star and meditate on its deeper significance we will feel the urge from the Spirit within to rise up and answer the WHAT, WHY, WHERE, HOW, and WHEN of the Star points -- to reclaim our status as Celestial Beings. We shall affirm the idea, "I am an eternal spirit, an image of God; my Celestial Self is awaiting recognition."

"I and my Father are one."
-John 10:30-

Our repeated affirmation of this will confirm its Truth. This realization and self-knowledge will inspire us to ascend further into the Higher Consciousness. It is the answer to all our questions - WHERE we came from, WHY we are here, WHEN we shall embark on our further quests, HOW we will do this, and WHAT we may become.

It is our mental and spiritual restlessness that leads us to our quest for Higher Consciousness. Our responses on that quest mold and prepare our future world, a world real both in substance and in its continuing, all-pervasive process of Truth-in-Creation.

We are now prepared to contemplate our vast potential. We must ask, "What do I really want?" Possible choices will appear in our minds in terms of Wholeness and Oneness in Eternity. We must also ask "Have we covered the requirements of Divine Order and Purpose?" These requirements are the Will to Life, the Will to Love, and the Will to Good.

The Will to Life - Awareness

What was the first cause of awareness? Perhaps it was the partaking of knowledge without wisdom, the indulging in mundane pleasures, the gratifying of the appetites of the body rather than of the soul. This first deviation from Divine Law set itself in opposition to the soul's original state of at-one-ment with God. The higher-order Will to Life is the desire to return to that initial state of Unity. The Quest for Return will be no quick or easy task; rather, it will require a steady effort. The means will be suggested by the study of our Stars of Destiny. Aided by the analysis of its five Points, we can improve ourselves and embark upon that Quest for Higher Consciousness.

The Will to Love

In our search for illumination, there comes a point of superseding ourselves, of rising above and beyond our former abilities and limitations, of realizing the greater talent within our souls. We can help ourselves reach that point by listening within for the suggestions of our higher selves .When we let the God of Love within do the work, we shall find a surer inner peace, a firmer faith, and a greater Path of Light for guidance. We have learned that we are Children of God, and that peace and harmony await us; we need only prepare ourselves properly to ask so that we might receive.

The Will to Good - God, the Superconscious Self

The Great Spiritual Truth exists in the Eternal Now,valid for all Ages and available to everyone. We are responsible for the kind of lives we live, for we have the knowledge of and can adhere to - the practices necessary to attain our goals. The Divine Plan and Purpose is to gain unity with God. We accomplish this through the renewal of mind through the transformation of Consciousness. We conceive of the future Life as the ascent of the self toward the unfolding Divine Self, as a change of mind and heart to a new higher and better state of consciousness.

We are now experiencing a period of great transition. Women and men will create great and inspirational art, music, and literature as natural expressions of our potential for advancement. We must seek the influence of such coming master-works as well as of both Sciences and Metaphysics in order to progress into the higher planes of existence that lie just ahead.

As we begin our journeys into these higher planes, we will begin to enjoy and look forward to further study and contemplation, for we are now ready and willing to seek the highest good. The positive spiritual way of life is genuinely practical as well as fulfilling. As we tune in to the Universal Rhythm, we will sense an infinite love and Divine guidance. We must prepare to have the unknown within us become consciously known and believed.

We may wonder if we are fantasizing beyond reality; rather, we should consider that such fantasies could be the Divine Truth about ourselves. We will discover our Higher Selves, selves latent but now emerging. These Selves have led us this far in our search for spirituality and in our studies of metaphysics. It has led us to find and analyze our Star of Destiny and it will guide us to greater new experiences.

We must determine to get the very best from this exciting exploration, and realize that we have fostered a goal of ascendance that is near at hand.

Amen.

Appendices

Appendix A

A Thirteen-Pointed Star?

How close are we to needing a Star of Thirteen Points to symbolize the potential for our future development?

In this book I have focused upon the Five-Pointed Pentacle as the Star of Destiny, the Star coming into particular prominence at this point in the development of our consciousness. I have also presented sketches of the characteristics of other Stars of many points, up to the Twelve-Pointed Star of Exaltation. But even now vibrations and harmonies of the Earth plane hint that we may in time attain consciousness even greater than that symbolized by the Twelve-Pointed Star. The path we have to travel is indeed an exciting one of great promise, and we shall come to activate Stars with an infinite number of points.

The number Thirteen resonates deeply in our consciousness. Its significance is reflected in both the changes we face each day and in the deep mysteries of our distant past.[1] It is only reasonable to assume that it will continue to influence our development in future ages.

The earliest appearance of the recognition of the power of the number Thirteen lies hidden far back in prehistory. Archaeological discoveries tell of pyramids all over the world. Many of them had thirteen steps to their summits. The ancient Mayans built thirteen such sacred pyramids in the Yucatan Peninsula. The Mayans are known by scientists and metaphysicians alike for their intricate calendar, which was based in part on the number Thirteen.[2]

Similar appreciation of the significance of Thirteen occurs in the pyramids of Egypt. These pyramids encode great mysteries and prophecies many of which are symbolically indicated in units of thirteen.

The number Thirteen plays an important part in Biblical symbology also. Jacob and his twelve sons and Jesus and His twelve disciples are just two examples of the powerful thirteen influence that permeates Biblical tradition.

Ancient mythology too, often resonates to Thirteen.

And it was the Greek mathematician and philosopher Pythagoras who began to systematize study of the hidden meanings of such numbers as Thirteen.

Our present-day civilization draws on all these ancient sources of knowledge. Our religious practices and institutions, our philosophical and ethical systems, our standards of science and mathematics, our music and literature, our legal and political structures - all these have built upon the important early traditions of the Bible, the various mythologies, and the Greek philosophers. We can truly say that the Thirteen influence that permeated these ancient cultures permeates us today as well.

Those of us in the United States of America are particularly attuned to the number Thirteen. We all know that our nation was originally formed from thirteen colonies and that our first flag had thirteen stars and thirteen stripes. The horoscope cast for the hour of the signing of the Declaration of Independence shows the Sun at 13 degrees of Cancer.

The Great Seal of the United States, which appears on the dollar bill, is also replete with reference to the number Thirteen. The eagle on its front side clutches thirteen arrows in its right claw and an olive branch with thirteen leaves and thirteen olives in its left claw. The eagle bears an arms with thirteen stripes and above it is a constellation of thirteen stars. Finally, the motto E pluribus unum (Out of many, one) contained thirteen letters.

The Seal's reverse side is equally rich in Thirteen symbology. For example, the pyramid has thirteen steps and the motto Annuit coeptis has thirteen letters.[3]

It appears obvious, then, that from the start the United States was designed to be a beacon of light, a source of great knowledge and good, a veritable cradle of liberty. This role in the world has only become more and more important throughout our history, and our responsibility to all the peoples of this world in our present Nuclear Age is immeasurable. This is our Manifest Destiny - to lead the world toward the Universal Consciousness.

This Destiny resonates in each of us in part through the influence of the number Thirteen, and will mark our lives in both the present and in the world beyond.

Thus while the full energy and benefit of a Thirteen-Pointed Star may lie far in our future it certainly seems to be a useful symbol for what we desire our Planet to become.

Thirteen-Pointed Star

We may only just now have developed a concrete means of analyzing even a Five-Pointed Star, and can only aspire to the energies of Stars of Six, Seven, Eight, or even Twelve Points, but the Thirteen-Pointed Star is part of our eventual Destiny, and, as we have seen, its seed already lies within us and can inspire us in our Quest.

This work and others indicates a renewed appreciation of the influence of the number Thirteen. The Thirteen-Pointed Star is thus a particularly appropriate symbol to inspire us and point us toward our future. This trend of recognition of the significance of Thirteen accords well with the coming New Age; it is one of the many signs that this Age is fast approaching. [4] To reflect this coming Age of brotherhood, of working toward our Manifest Destiny of Universal Consciousness, some have suggested that we adopt a new Universal Calendar. Interestingly, that calendar is also attuned to the number Thirteen.

The Universal Calendar would consist of thirteen months of twenty-eight days. Each month would in turn consist of four seven-day weeks. Because month and week divisions coincide each date would fall on the same day of the week each month.

SAMPLE MONTH						
SUN	MON	TUES	WED	THUR	FRI	SAT
1	2	3	4	5	6	7
8	9	10	11	12	13	14
15	16	17	18	19	20	21
22	23	24	25	26	27	28

With thirteen twenty-eight day months, the Universal Calendar year would total 364 days. The necessary extra day could be a New Year's Day falling outside of any month. Dates for holidays could be permanently set - Christmas could always be the last Wednesday of December, Easter might be the last Sunday in April, and other holidays could be scheduled to fall regularly on Mondays (a change we have already begun to institute).

The many advantages that can accrue by an adoption of this Universal Calendar are obvious. It can add ease to all manner of planning. It will be of particular use in commercial affairs. It could replace the various different calendars that divide the world today. And it would thus promote the unity we all should aspire to. It is thus an appropriate emblem for our future.

As markers of time, calendars have been reflections of the civilizations that use them. Each civilization adjusts its calendar differently. Adjustment was necessary because agricultural and religious needs led ancient people to refer to the movement of both the Sun and the Moon. The Solar year and the Lunar Year, however, are of different durations. Thus, it is a challenge to synthesize in a single calendar each fundamental measure of time - the day (the Earth's rotation on its axis in reference to the Sun), the month (the Moon's revolution around the Earth), and the year (the Earth's revolution around the Sun). However a calendar is arranged, the Vernal, or Spring Equinox must fall on the same day every year.

Primitive people had to adjust their calendars nearly every year. In the days of Rome, the calendar was a lunar based calendar. When Julius Caesar conquered Egypt, he observed the greater accuracy of the Egyptians solar-based calendar. He borrowed from the Egyptian calendar to reform the Roman Calendar, and in 46 B.C. established a new beginning to the year, the standard lengths of the months, and regulations for leap years. The resulting calendar is called the Julian Calendar.

The Julian Calendar was a great improvement over the old Roman Calendar, but it was still inaccurate. It was based on a solar year of 365¼ days, but as ¼ is still an approximation, the calendar over time became further and further off base.

In 1582, Pope Gregory XIII reformed the Julian Calendar by dropping ten days from that year to bring it back to the correct cycle. But as this was the time of the Protestant Reformation, not all countries adopted the Gregorian, or New Style, Calendar. England did not adopt the reform until 1752, (The United States likewise adopted the Gregorian Calendar that year, for it was still an English colony.)

The Gregorian Calendar is the one used today in the Western World and indeed throughout most of the entire world. Although many other calendars still exist, the Gregorian Calendar is used in most of the world's commerce and communication.

As you can see, each change in our calendar has reflected a changing world - a world ever more technologically accomplished and ever more unified in communication, travel, and consciousness.

It is time, perhaps, to consider seriously another calendar reform. We deserve a Universal Calendar that resonates with the powers of the number Thirteen, one that can help unify the world and propel us ever forward.

1. For deeper treatment of the significance of the number Thirteen, consult *Thirteen: Birth or Death?* Faith Javane and Dusty Bunker, Association for Inner Development, Hampton, NH, 1976.

2. For an extensive discussion of the Mayan calendrical and numerical systems consult *The Mayan Factor: Path Beyond Technology*, José Argüelles, Bear and Company, Santa Fe, NM, 1987.

3. The detail and depth of these and other symbols in our Seal have been thoroughly described by Paul Foster Case, who attributes the design of these symbols to men versed in the Masonic mysteries. Consult *The Great Seal of the United States: Its History, Symbolism, and Message for the New Age*, JF. Rowny Press, Santa Barbara, CA, 1935.

4. For an astrological analysis of the approach to this New Age, see Appendix B, "New World Mutations and The Coming Aquarian Age."

Appendix B

New World Mutations

The Coming Aquarian Age

Because we do not know the birth date of the Planet Earth, we do not have a Horoscope for it. We do however, have a Chart which shows the Earth's destiny. This Chart is erected by what is known as a New World Mutation.

A New World Mutation occurs when Jupiter and Saturn are conjunct. Jupiter-Saturn Conjunctions occur in cycles, with each cycle consisting of Conjunctions in a particular Element. In general, the first of a continuous series of these Conjunctions in an Element is called a New World Mutation, or Great Mutation. Following a New World Mutation, Jupiter and Saturn make a cycle of other Conjunctions in the same Element, about once every twenty years.

Conjunctions of Jupiter and Saturn often indicate important events. New World Mutations mark particularly significant turning points in Earth's history. These Conjunctions and Mutations thus reveal many facets of the development of humanity on Earth, and can be said to serve as Horoscopes for the Planet.

The following Tables show the births of great teachers of the past that have occured during Jupiter-Saturn Conjunctions, as well as dates of recent and coming Conjunctions and Mutations.

Table I
Selected Past Jupiter-Saturn Conjunctions and the Births of Great Teachers

Date	Conjunction	Great Teachers
B.C.		
662	(in Sagittarius)	—Zoroaster, taught the wisdom of astrology
563	(in Taurus)	—Buddha, taught practical common sense
384	(in Gemini)	—Aristotle, taught higher knowledge
7	(in Pisces)	—Jesus, taught love and forgiveness
A.D.		
570	(in Libra)	—Mohammed, taught balance and justice
1821	(in Aries)	—Mary Baker Eddy, taught healing and religious service

Table II

Recent and Upcoming Jupiter-Saturn Conjunctions

Earth Conjunctions Cycle

Date	Conjunction
1842	(in Capricorn) -New World Mutation in Earth
1861	(in Virgo)
1881	(in Taurus)
1901	(in Capricorn)
1921	(in Virgo)
1940	(in Taurus)
1961	(in Capricorn)

Transition Period

1980/81 (in Libra)	-	First Conjunctions in Air
2000 (in Taurus)		
2020 (in Capricorn)	-	Final Con junction in Earth

Air Conjunctions Cycle

2020 (in Aquarius)	-	New World Mutation in Air Beginning of AGE OF AQUARIUS

Between each Cycle of Jupiter-Saturn Conjunctions is a period of transition, as you can see from Table II. The Earth has lived in an Earth Conjunctions Cycle since 1842. In 1980 and 1981 it witnessed several Jupiter-Saturn Conjunctions in the Air Sign Libra - the first harbingers of a New Air Age. Yet we will have further Jupiter-Saturn Conjunctions in Earth Signs before we finally experience the New World Mutation in Air in 2020 - the actual beginning of the Air Conjunctions Cycle, of the Age of Aquarius.

This great and hopeful transition from an Earth Conjunctions Cycle to an Air Conjunctions Cycle is truly the story of our times. Let us, then explore it in some greater detail. The following charts are displayed on the Natural Zodiac.

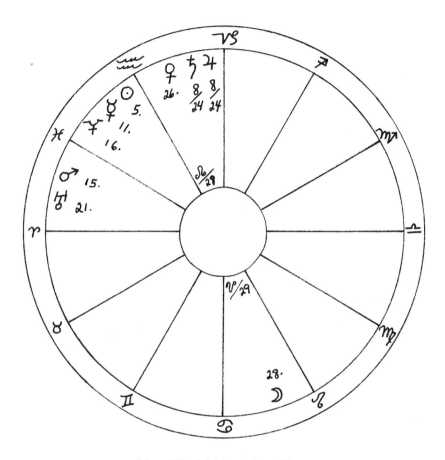

New World Mutation Chart

January 26, 1842[1]

1. Pluto is not shown in this Chart because it was not discovered until 1930.

The period since the New World Mutation in Earth has seen tremendous change. The Industrial Revolution ushered in a period of amazing technological progress. All that we take for granted today - electricity, the radio, the telephone, television, the automobile, the airplane, and even such wonders as computers and space flight - have been developed during this Earth Cycle. The Earth Cycle has also brought great achievements in business like the creation of huge companies with unimaginably vast resources and power. And fantastic scientific and medical advances have contributed much to our health and longevity. In short, we have seen the standard of living improve throughout the world - rapidly in the advanced nations and steadily, albeit more slowly, in developing nations.

And yet this Cycle of great material progress has also clearly shown the dangers of focusing on material concerns to the exclusion of more spiritual ones. The commercial acumen that we have developed and all our resulting economic advances have too often led us to adopt extremely competitive, callous, miserly, and shallow natures and have fostered societies marked by an ever-widening gap between the rich and the poor. And the technological knowledge that has given us such daily comfort has also given us great weapons of war and destruction, which we have turned upon ourselves time and time again. The development of nuclear power and now nuclear weapons has exponentially deepened the dangers we face.

Humanity is becoming more aware of the many dangers arising from a concentration on our material side. We have seen in the last several decades an increased concern with civil rights, women's rights, and human rights. We have sought detente and then arms control and now arms reduction agreements with our "enemies." And we are, increasingly mindful of those less fortunate than ourselves be they the homeless of our own cities or the starving masses of the Third World. Clearly, "something is in the Air."

What we are experiencing is a first taste of the Air Age of Aquarius. The 1980's began with the first Jupiter-Saturn Conjunction in Air as a herald of that Age. This Conjunction occured in the Sign Libra, which reveals that we live in a time of a new and balancing vibration, a vibration that will prepare us for the full flower of the coming Age.

The year 1981 was a most significant one in our history. It began with the end of the traumatizing ordeal of the American hostages. The seizure of the hostages showed us how fortunate and civilized we are in comparison with the conditions and behavior of other nations. It also reminded us that we must tend to our standing in the world around us. We could no longer retreat from a greater destiny that demanded attention to the entire planet.

And at almost the same time as the hostage release, Ronald Reagan was inaugurated as President.[2] His election had been a significant departure from political trends of the previous two

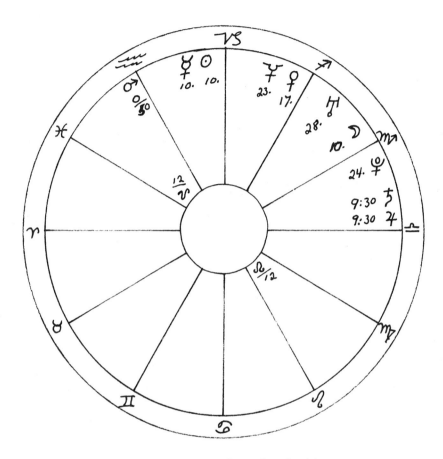

Forerunner Conjunction in Air

January 1, 1981

decades and the Reagan presidency marked a great change in America's direction. It witnessed a revitalization of American patriotism at home and prestige abroad. It saw the world's two greatest powers begin a sincere dialogue with the stated goal of *eliminating* some of their more terrifying weapons systems. And it brought on increased attention to our greater quality of life, with education, the environment, and the care of the underprivileged higher on the national agenda than they had been in some time.

Yet these many advances since 1981 have often come in the arena of concern and discussion rather than in that of concrete result. We have clearly not yet arrived in the New Age. We are just beginning to "shift gears" from a time focusing on our physical and material selves to a time focusing more on our intellectual and spiritual natures.

An examination of two Charts which will be active before the Earth comes under the full-fledged influence of the New Age indicates exciting trends and great changes. These "Signs in the Heavens" mark the beginning of a new era.

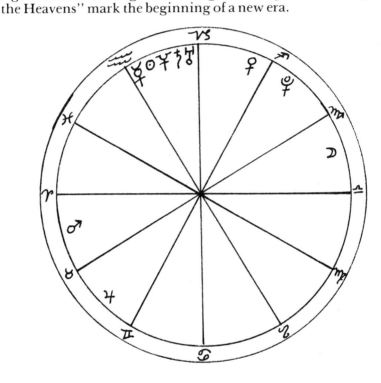

January 1, 1989

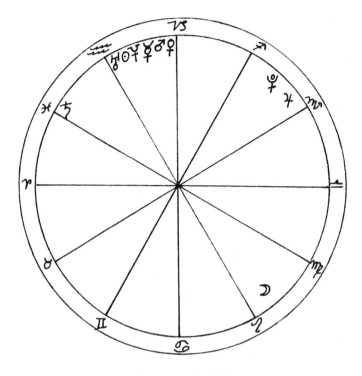

January 1, 1994

The Charts for January 1, 1989 and for January 1, 1994 show a line-up of Planets conjuncting in the Sign Capricorn. These powerful Aspects indicate many turning points and could even suggest a new form of government, for Capricorn is a governmental Sign. Saturn-ruled Capricorn connotes the discipline needed in all mundane situations. Saturn moves slowly but forces its way with great power and control.[3]

The last Jupiter-Saturn Conjunction in Earth will take place on December 16, 2020. Just six days later, December 22, 2020, Jupiter and Saturn will make their first Conjunction in Aquarius. This is a New World Mutation, and can be interpreted as the actual beginning of the long-awaited and long-prepared-for Aquarian Age.

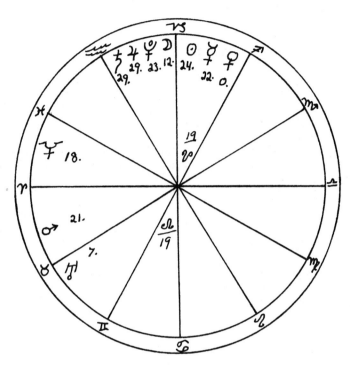

Final Conjunction in Earth

December 16, 2020

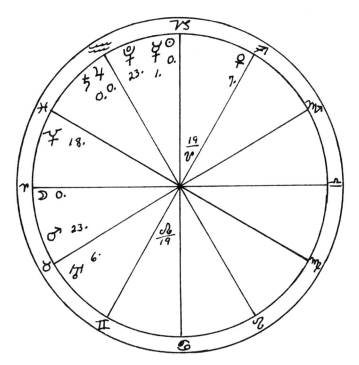

New World Mutation in Air

December 22, 2020

The Age of Aquarius will bring a new order and a new philosophy strongly influenced by the nature of Aquarius's ruling Planet Uranus, called The Awakener. This influence will inspire in humanity the desire for service to others, to the community, and to the world. This will be an Age of brotherhood and peace, a time truly to realize and actualize "I am my brother's keeper."

The hope for the Aquarian Age is that the head and heart will join in partnership to build a better world of Wholeness. We hope to experience a more compassionate and stimulating creativity among all people and a greater out-flow of spiritual force for a harmonious world. We can dedicate ourselves as souls to manifesting a new attitude toward the future.

The Divine Plan conceives of the future as the Ascent of Man. The Divine Purpose is to return to God-consciousness. These Charts help confirm that such a destiny does indeed lie in store for us.

Appendix C
Esoteric Numerology

The Metaphysical Sciences furnish signs and symbols representing the plan for the mental and physical regeneration of each individual back toward the concept of God-hood - the image in which each of us was created.

When we grow weary of the glamor and temptations of a mundane lifestyle, inspiration for a greater and more meaningful type of life takes over and we seek a better outlook. God gave us free-will and we fearlessly step out into manifestation.

Our spiritual anatomy follows the rhythms in Nature with a teleological pattern, a design keyed to unlimited progress. We grow from Helios (Sun-centered) to Teleos (infinity-centered) - with the end result to be Cosmic Consciousness.

To foster this growth we must harness the energies of Nature. These energies are constantly radiated to us from our Names and Birthdates and thus underlie the powers of the odd and even numbers that Esoteric Numerology helps us understand.

These energies are broadly expansive, even beyond the division of sex. In the Aquarian Age the balance between the male and female energies are rising to gain their long lost equality. In this Age energies will be equal as they should be. Your Name vibrates with energy that shows what you are. The total of your birth Month, Day and Year show qualities to be developed. Odd Numbers forge ahead; Even Numbers smooth the way.

What follows is a short list of vibrational responses to the Numbers that we can derive from our Names and Birthdates. Higher qualities are given to encourage responses of a positive nature. Whether our Numbers be odd or even, our responses can always be in accordance to our own *Humanity*.

1. This number becomes a leader, the first to try new ideas, for the ego-self is built and ready to learn new concepts. It represents a starting point, unity, Oneness, a time for new beginnings and for the coming of great events in Human History.

> Behold - I make all things new."

> -Rev. 21: 5-

2. This number is aware of possessions, especially of values in whatever form, and learns both the importance of caring for the body on Earth and consideration for others (me, and not me). It represents choices, cooperation, pairs of opposites, duality.

3. This number develops peace and poise through imagination and thus must learn to concentrate. It represents expansion, a scattering of forces and the Trinity. Under this number social graces become beneficial and Divinity reveals itself.

4. This number is honest and sensible, a square shooter, accurate and efficient, stable, a builder of character and four-square conduct.

5. This number is one of progressive and changing attitudes, accepting positive challenges as different adventures in life provide work towards freedom of action. It has the ability to choose the true from the false.

6. This number is a harmonizer, poised and protective of others, a home maker who is contented with loving service to family, and a guardian who shields others from harm.

7. This number is introspective, exclusive, fastidious, and meditative, a quiet thinker who cares calmly for people and circumstances and tries for perfection.

8. This number is dignified, self-reliant, and executive, and has a penetrating insight into other forces. It represents responsibility taken seriously and management situations conducted justly and firmly.

9. This number is the Humanitarian offering service to others and to the universe as a whole. It represents Universality, love, and understanding.

10. This number represents the time for outgrowing material desires and moving onward to Spiritual attainments. It is a combination of the ego of "I" and the Divinity of "0."

Let the Christ be formed in you.

-Galatians 4:19-

For further information on the Spiritual meanings of numbers, consult F. Javane and D. Bunker, *Numerology and The Divine Triangle*, Whitford Press, West Chester, PA, 1979.

2. Ronald Reagan was born in Aquarius, an Air Sign ruled by Uranus "The Awakener." His successor George Bush was also born under an Air Sign - Gemini, ruled by the intellectual Mercury.

3. More detailed astrological analysis can reveal even further characteristics of the coming Aquarian Age.